ROUTLEDGE LIBRARY EDITIONS: SCOTLAND

Volume 15

THE LION AND THE UNICORN

THE LION AND THE UNICORN
What England Has Meant to Scotland

ERIC LINKLATER

LONDON AND NEW YORK

First published in 1935 by George Routledge & Sons Ltd.

This edition first published in 2022
by Routledge
2 Park Square, Milton Park, Abingdon, Oxon OX14 4RN

and by Routledge
605 Third Avenue, New York, NY 10158

Routledge is an imprint of the Taylor & Francis Group, an informa business

© 1935 Eric Linklater

All rights reserved. No part of this book may be reprinted or reproduced or utilised in any form or by any electronic, mechanical, or other means, now known or hereafter invented, including photocopying and recording, or in any information storage or retrieval system, without permission in writing from the publishers.

Trademark notice: Product or corporate names may be trademarks or registered trademarks, and are used only for identification and explanation without intent to infringe.

British Library Cataloguing in Publication Data
A catalogue record for this book is available from the British Library

ISBN: 978-1-03-206184-9 (Set)
ISBN: 978-1-00-321338-3 (Set) (ebk)
ISBN: 978-1-03-207920-2 (Volume 15) (hbk)
ISBN: 978-1-03-207944-8 (Volume 15) (pbk)
ISBN: 978-1-00-321210-2 (Volume 15) (ebk)

DOI: 10.4324/9781003212102

Publisher's Note
The publisher has gone to great lengths to ensure the quality of this reprint but points out that some imperfections in the original copies may be apparent.

Disclaimer
The publisher has made every effort to trace copyright holders and would welcome correspondence from those they have been unable to trace.

THE LION & THE UNICORN

or

WHAT ENGLAND HAS
MEANT TO SCOTLAND

by

ERIC LINKLATER

GEORGE ROUTLEDGE
AND SONS, LTD. Broadway
House, Carter Lane, London, E.C.
1935

First published 1935

PRINTED IN GREAT BRITAIN BY THE EDINBURGH PRESS, EDINBURGH AND LONDON

To the Memory of
LEWIS GRASSIC GIBBON
Who asked Me to Write
This Book

CONTENTS

CHAP.		PAGE
I. Prelude in the First Person Singular		11
II. Roundabout and Swings		35
III. The Kirk of Scotland		53
IV. The Dark Ages		79
V. Addenda and Corrigenda		95
VI. The Question of Culture		107
VII. Bibulous Interlude		137
VIII. To-day and To-morrow		147
IX. The Tentative Conclusion		179

I
PRELUDE IN THE FIRST PERSON SINGULAR

I
PRELUDE IN THE FIRST PERSON SINGULAR

It was entirely by chance that I opened the 1933 edition of the Medical Directory at page 1236. It was by chance, by the fortuitous pull of certain small muscles of the eye—called, I think, the superior or inferior recti—that I happened to notice, near the top of the page, the words Glasgow and Aberdeen and Edinburgh. But chance having opened the door, curiosity stepped inside and hung up his hat: to be plain and straightforward, as current use prefers, I counted the number of doctors who, having graduated in a Scottish university, were now practising in England. There were twelve; and the total number of names on the page was twenty-six.

The immediate inference, however, was unjustifiable. It was too early to conclude that out of every thirteen doctors in England, six were Scots: because graduates of a Scottish university are not necessarily Scots by birth or blood—Edinburgh is notoriously attractive to exotics—and because other pages of the Directory might show a very different ratio.

I turned, again by chance, to page 488. It contained thirty-two names, of which eight were those of Scots, or Scottish graduates, practising in England. This brought the proportion down to one in four. I made a similar calculation on page 726, and found a ratio of seven to nineteen. But on page 924 it became alarmingly four to one: four Scots to one Englishman. This page, however, was a catalogue of Macdonalds: there was no room for English names among these descendants of the mountain clan, these survivors of the Penal Acts: and reading their brave patronymics I forgot for a while that I was hunting a ratio, and began to make in my mind pretty pictures of social evolution. For the grandfathers of many of these gentlemen whose names lay before me—and whose Austin motor-cars were everywhere aggravating the traffic problem, whose wives, at that very moment, were arranging fine flowers in their drawing-rooms—their grandfathers, I say, had been poor men in a plaid, with a black hillside for their morning view and a handful of meal for their dinner, and their grandfathers' great-grandfathers had fought at Inverlochy under the Great

PRELUDE IN THE FIRST PERSON SINGULAR

Marquis, and died no doubt, like MacTavish in the song, with a dirk in their bowels. But their grandsons, whose names I was studying, had put away their skean dhus, and carrying bistoury and forceps instead, were bleeding their English neighbours more profitably than anyone since the Black Douglas.

England, or so it seemed from the evidence before me, was for Scots, or at any rate for Scottish doctors, a land of opportunity, a happy Canaan where panel patients grew in every tree. I returned to my statistics and came to the conclusion—though I am no actuary—that our surgeons and physicians had amply revenged Prince Charles Edward's retreat from Derby.

From history to geography is but a little step, and turning to a map I considered those large extensions of England, those bright-red areas—benignly red, as different from the squalid hue of Communism as arterial blood from the unclean venous flow—and thought for a little while of the enlargement that Scotsmen had found therein, from Manitoba to New Zealand, from Rhodesia to Singapore. Not doctors only had followed King James VI into the land of Canaan, but farmers, engineers, administrators, soldiers, clerks and contractors had all been enriched by the Union of the Crowns and the Sabine Marriage of the

Parliaments. Even Scottish novelists had benefited by those conjugations. But I was not so blind that I could not see the other side of the picture: if the partnership had been profitable for Scots, so also had it been profitable for England. Our political alliance may be an example of that mutually beneficent association that biologists call *symbiosis*; of which another illustration is the mycorhiza or fungus-root. 'It seems that the fungus draws nourishment from the tree-root, and that, in return, it passes into it, from the soil, water and salts, and also makes available the insoluble organic nitrogen-compounds present in leaf-mould and humus. Neither partner is absolutely dependent on the other; tree and fungus can be grown apart. But in Nature the solitary fungus does not fruit, and the uninfected tree grows less well than when it is provided with mycorhiza. This is an example of symbiosis, or living together to mutual benefit, notable because the two partners belong to such widely different classes of plants.'[1]

If this comparison has much foundation in fact, one may understand the angry impatience with which so many Scots reject the proposals of Scottish Nationalists. For the intention, or at least the hope, of the Scottish

[1] Sir J. Arthur Thomson.

PRELUDE IN THE FIRST PERSON SINGULAR

Nationalists is to dissolve the partnership with England. In England their aspirations arouse no great excitement, for though an intellectual minority, interested in political self-determination, mildly applauds them, the majority is happily ignorant of their existence. In Scotland, however, the Nationalist not seldom finds that even the gentlest enunciation of his faith awakes indignant anger. The solid advocate of the *status quo*, the warm Conservative, the canny businessman, will rise vicious as a plump holiday-maker, sleeping in the sun and startled by a raiding wasp, when he hears the conscientious buzzing of a Home Ruler. His attitude, indeed, the angry darting of his eyes, the impatient thrusting of his hand, may very closely resemble the appearance and the movements of a man roused from comfortable sleep; and Nationalists, like other reformers, believe there is merit in waking people up. But the advocate of the *status quo* may be justified in his anger: his sleep, which is contentment, may be a right and proper increment of the symbiosis.

Symbiosis, however, despite its advantages, is not necessarily an equal partnership. The unicellular plants called Algæ are adopted by tiny marine creatures called Radiolarians, whose nitrogenous waste they

PRELUDE IN THE FIRST PERSON SINGULAR

consume and for whom they liberate oxygen: but in time of crisis the Radiolarian may digest its Algæ. There are Scottish Nationalists, hypersensitive perhaps, who claim that Scotland is presently suffering such a digestive process. On the other hand there are certain cuttlefish that shine with a splendour not their own, but the gleam of friendly bacteria that cover their skin.[1] And there are critics, not necessarily unfriendly to Scotland, who think that Scotland's fame in the world is largely due to its association with England. Here, at its least estimate, is matter for argument.

But I do not mean to say too much about Scottish Nationalism. In such a study as this it would be an affectation of judicial ignorance to ignore entirely the existence of the movement, but I have no intention of elaborating a case for it either in the manner of a defending counsel or a prosecuting counsel. I hope to discuss, I fear discursively rather than profoundly, the historical relations and the cultural exchange of the two countries, and though my qualifications as an historian are regrettably slight—for I have neither the training nor the meticulous and persistent industry necessary for such a title—yet I am not quite so bad

[1] Again I owe my information to Sir J. Arthur Thomson.

an historian as some people have said. When, for example, I wrote a short biography of Mary, Queen of Scots, and offered a brand-new interpretation of her character, there were critics, not a few, who charged me with having concocted an hypothesis and cooked the evidence to suit it. This was not the case, though it might have been. For I did indeed begin with an hypothesis, and when the essay was half finished I was forced to destroy the one, reject the other, and start again. I had begun, lazily enough, with a modified Swinburnian theory of Mary as the Tragic Lover, and it was not until I had written or planned the greater part of the book that I heard the evidence calling me a liar. This was intensely annoying, because in the first place it was clear that I would have to do a lot more work—whereas I dote on idleness—and in the second place, though 'Liar!' was plain enough, it was far from clear what else the evidence was saying. Then, it happened, I fell into conversation with one of Mary's Catholic apologists, who argued learnedly and hotly to prove her a good candidate for canonization. So I read the evidence again, which the Catholic light did not wholly illuminate, but lit in part. Mary was no wanton: so much was clear. But neither was she innocent,

PRELUDE IN THE FIRST PERSON SINGULAR

except in the technical sense in which moralists use the word. The evidence now began to mutter, and repaying the courtesy of close attention, at last spoke clearly: Mary, it said, was a dynastical politician—in the sixteenth century the visiting moon can have found nothing remarkable in that—and she abstained from taking lovers for the sufficient reason that she found no great pleasure in love.

That was how *Mary, Queen of Scots*, came to have its shape and content, and I tell the story as a kind of promise or indication that, having once been honest, I shall try to be honest again. I do not go so far as to say that honesty is a habit ingrained: yet I am not wholly a stranger to it: and in this matter of Anglo-Scottish relations I hope to be honest for my own sake, and come to an honest conclusion, for I have been greatly troubled by the problem, and a clear understanding is a comfort to the mind.

I have, moreover, a couple of qualifications, both accidental, for the task ahead of me. I have no hereditary bias. One quarter of my blood is English, for my maternal grandmother, whom I dearly loved and whose memory I adore, was English out of Northamptonshire; and in the rest of me there is no racial memory of Culloden, the Clearances, or other

PRELUDE IN THE FIRST PERSON SINGULAR

such things that still trouble the thoughts of many Highlanders. For on my father's side my ancestry, happily undistinguished, is of Orkney, and in Orkney we felt nothing of the English wars except a good deal of the press-gang in Napoleonic times. Our tyrants, indeed, were Stewarts, a couple of ogrish Earls with a taste for architecture and the *corvée*, who successfully reduced the Islands to ruin for two centuries.—Mr Storer Clouston, the historian of Orkney, has truly said that Orkney never derived any benefit from its association with Scotland till Scottish authority was swallowed by England.—It is true that I prefer to live in Scotland, but that is because I think its climate and scenery are better than those of England: I like clear streams and the bright Atlantic waves. But a preference, even eager preference, for the diamond clarity and the curving rush of a Highland river, for the noise and the colour of a western beach, does not necessarily bias one's political, historical, or sociological opinions. Heaven knows they are biassed enough by other things.

My claim to a faculty of impartial judgment does not, indeed, go very far. I am, as I have said, free from racial prejudice. But I have a score of violent intellectual prejudices. I hate Fascism, Communism,

PRELUDE IN THE FIRST PERSON SINGULAR

and all other political or economic systems that cripple and reduce the stature of individual men for the mythical benefit of an imaginary totality. I hate puritanism, teetotalism, and the mental deformity that produces them. I hate stupidity in high places, and only of necessity condone it in myself. I cannot believe that rationalization of industry, television, and the power to fly to Australia in three days are irrefutable proof of human progress: if progress be nothing more than these, let me fire, though silently, the second barrel of the gun with which Mr Ford once startled the world. 'History is Bunk,' said Mr Ford: 'Progress is Hooey,' I reply. But my prejudices, which often lie on me as a monstrous load of debt, have sometimes relief in Time, which, like an ever-rolling stream, bears all his duns away. I exercise the purely human privilege of changing my mind, that is. There was a time, for instance, when I hated pacifism; and now I hate militarism. But this, perhaps, is a variant of my hatred of stupidity in high places, for the cruelty of modern war is a minor complaint beside its unmitigated fatuity. At any rate, if my disquisition brings me within reaching distance of any of these matters, I cannot promise fair play. There are some things which do not deserve fair play.

PRELUDE IN THE FIRST PERSON SINGULAR

So much talk of stupidity reminds me, *per contra*, of a major argument in the Scottish Nationalists' battery—I promised to leave these people in the background, but I cannot help marching them to the front for another minute or two—and that is the way in which all recent governments have neglected the Scottish fishermen.[1] I am not, for the moment, concerned with the humanitarian aspect of this neglect. I am more perturbed by its folly. Surely, to a Conservative at least, the national value of the fishermen should be apparent? The Conservative mind is never forgetful of the problem of national defence; and it is only a few years since we emerged from a war in which the fishermen played a more arduous, heroic, and necessary part than anyone except the infantry and the gunners of the front line. Even in time of peace a fisherman is not without value, and in time of war the crew of a drifter is worth much more than a squadron of Life Guards. From the Conservative point of view the fishermen deserve to be treated, not merely with decency, but with lavish and unceasing generosity. They should be pampered

[1] The current Herring Industry Bill, though unduly delayed, may be helpful in some degree; but as it largely consists of Rationalization suspicion is aroused that it is more concerned with the profits of the industry than with its personnel.

and cossetted and made much of. They should be loved, and applauded, and encouraged to multiply. But instead of this they are handicapped by mean and ineffectual legislation, their harbours are allowed to fall into ruin, their shameful poverty is driving them off the sea. In many parts of Scotland the inshore fishing is dead. Elsewhere it is dying. And the drifters have scarcely so good a title to that name as their elected legislators. Yet fishermen, in time of war, become mine-sweepers and necessarily reinforce the Royal Navy, whose honour, if not an anchor as well, is laudably tattooed on every Conservative breast. Why, then, do Conservatives so neglect our fishermen? The more rabid kind of Nationalist would answer, 'Because the fishing industry is mainly a Scottish industry, and the Westminster Parliament, being predominantly an English institution, is ignorant of its circumstances and careless of its fate.' But I, broader-minded and more charitable, cannot acquiesce in such a view. The only reasonable explanation that I can find is *Quos Deus vult perdere prius dementat.*

The amiable sceptic might well reply to this accusation of neglect that even a Scottish Parliament might refuse to treat the fishermen as handsomely as I, for example, think desirable. He might suggest, not impertinently, that a Scottish Parliament would be so dominated by the industrial and commercial interests of the Scottish Midlands as to have little time left in which to consider the welfare of the Moray Firth. And this possibility cannot be denied, especially by anyone who believes in history's power of repetition: for Scotland's rulers in the past were habitually men with the bigoted self-interest of a suckling, and such lack of conscience as would startle the keeper of a bawdy-house.—In comparison with the Scottish nobility of Queen Mary's time, or with Highland lairds in the Eighteenth Century, Mr Baldwin's government of to-day is a regiment of God's holy and immaculate angels.—Democracy, however, and their own folly have killed the old aristocracy; and whatever tendency to self-interest, or sectional interest, there might be in a Scottish Parliament of to-morrow, would be offset by its proximity, in so small a country, to the areas of dissatisfaction. A Parliamentary lobby is vulnerable to pressure in inverse proportion to the square of its distance from the seat of discontent.

It may be admitted, however, that a Scottish Nationalist is something like a man who goes to a racecourse and sees two horses in the paddock: one, called *Status Quo*, has only three legs, and the other, called *Home Rule*, is so draped in long stable-cloths that no one can tell whether he has any legs at all: yet the Nationalist, basing his decision on idealism, probability, and the dubious record of the stud-book, boldly puts his money on the latter.

My attention, this evening, was attracted by a newspaper contents bill.—It is the fifth day of February and I am living and writing in Aberdeen, a handsome city once notable for learning, and still the circumvallation of a respectable university.—A newsboy, representing our local evening paper, carried a poster that declared: 'Aberdeen Woman Shoplifter Sentenced.' Now it seemed to me that an educated and intelligent stranger would be sadly puzzled by this. He would know, being educated, that the population of Aberdeen was about 160,000. He would remember that the University of Aberdeen was founded in 1498, and being intelligent he would suppose the people of Aberdeen, born in its academic shade, to be keenly interested in Culture and the Best Things. And knowing so much he would be hard put to it to guess why a tale about an unknown female shoplifter should be effective in persuading so many people—with Cultural and Intellectual Interests

PRELUDE IN THE FIRST PERSON SINGULAR

—to buy an evening paper. He would refuse to believe that so slight a matter, a matter to excite poor pelting villages but nothing greater, could entertain so large and cultured a population. He would look desperately for the news in this story of petty pilfering. And his deduction, his only possible deduction, would be that the operative word was *Sentenced*. He would conclude that all Aberdeen women were habitual shoplifters, and the news of the story lay in the fact that one of them had, at last, been caught, tried, and convicted.

But alas for the intelligent stranger! He has guessed wrong. The sub-editors of the Aberdeen evening paper know their trade, and they would not plaster their contents bills with village gossip if village gossip were not to the city's taste. A parochial taste? It is the penalty of provincialism. And the remedy? To reduce the degree of provincialism by restoring Scotland's national status and re-establishing its government in Edinburgh.

Having said this, I shrink from the abuse of economists, practical men, good common-sensibles. I hear them howling with hatred and derision. I would split the United Kingdom in two, for no larger reason than the giving to Aberdeen of something better to think about than the apprehension of female shoplifters? Lunacy, they say. They crack their cheeks, they scornfully cachinnate. But in spite of their laughter I may be in the right of it, and they, the economists and sound commercial brethren, may be hopelessly at fault and abominable heretics. Their criterion of merit is ' Will it pay? ' What they mean by that word is not quite clear, for many businesses can be made to ' pay ' by sacking half the employees, who improbably derive much satisfaction from reading about the resulting profits. . . . But the Practical Man is coming to life. Let him speak for himself:

PRACTICAL MAN. You must admit that you have been talking rubbish. With no more evidence than a casual poster, and after a very tedious discussion of it, you assume that Aberdeen has a parochial mind. You imply, I suppose, that the rest of Scotland is no better. And you suggest that this state of affairs—if it exists—could be ameliorated by establishing an independent Scottish Government in Edinburgh. Does that mean that you believe people can be made to think higher thoughts by Act of Parliament?

LINKLATER. No. But I believe people degenerate when they lose control of their own affairs, and, as a corollary, that resumption of control may induce regeneration. To any nation the essential vitamin is responsibility.

PRACTICAL MAN. The words are excellent words, but I doubt if they mean much. I grant you there is a lamentable number of unemployed in Scotland, but apart from them our people are healthier, more prosperous, and more reasonably happy than they have ever been before. We have all the advantages of partnership in what is still the greatest power in the world, and I fail to see how you could wish for any larger responsibility than that.

LINKLATER. I don't. I want a smaller responsibility. With the best will in the world I can't persuade myself that I am responsible for the Commonwealth of British Nations, with all its surrounding colonies, dependencies, and mandated territories. But in a small country like Scotland——

PRACTICAL MAN. You would feel an exhilarating sense of responsibility for the upkeep of the parish pump. And do you think you would make a good caretaker for that useful engine? It would be a whole-time job, for if you removed English control from our affairs we would relapse into primitive competition, and Campbells and Macdonalds, Catholics and Presbyterians, Glasgow and Edinburgh, would all be fighting with each other for your pump-handle.

LINKLATER. That is most unlikely. We have outgrown these wasteful rivalries.

PRACTICAL MAN. Have you ever been to a football match between the Glasgow Rangers and the Celtic?

PRELUDE IN THE FIRST PERSON SINGULAR

If it weren't for the police every one of them would be a bloody battle.

LINKLATER. But we Nationalists have no intention of abolishing the police.

PRACTICAL MAN. No, but under Home Rule you mightn't be able to afford to pay them.

LINKLATER. There you go again! I tell you there are more important things than your everlasting preoccupation with profit and loss.

PRACTICAL MAN. I believe you are now on the point of talking about the Soul of Man.

LINKLATER (*testily*). What if I am?

PRACTICAL MAN. I shall be most interested to hear what you have to say about it. I myself am reasonably fond of my fellow men, but I have no great opinion of them. The vast majority want nothing more than physical comfort, and even the superior few, the artists and the architects of society, need security, such as I promote, but which you would shatter.

LINKLATER. You stand for comfort and security, you say. But there are millions of people, in Great Britain alone, who live without any comfort at all, and security—spiritual security, at any rate—is equally a stranger to those whom you call the superior few. Therefore the system, of which you are a part and which you defend, has manifestly failed to do even what you say it should do. That is because it has outgrown its strength. It has become so enormous that no one can possibly understand its whole machinery, or legislate for its aggregate good, because its aggregate is composed of too many irreconcilable minorities. The remedy, therefore, is to subdivide it, and reorganize the units of that division, not for the profit of a few, but for the welfare of each majority: and by welfare I mean the opportunity to lead a full life, a fully conscious life, a life of adequate responsibility, a life in which work and leisure are fairly mingled, a life in which there is proper hope of reward for individual merit, a life in which there is room to sympathize with, and make allowance for, individual frailties. You may talk as long as you please about the economic arguments against such a division: economy is a good servant, but a bad master. You may preach for ever about the industrial inefficiency of small units: efficiency has no meaning unless it means the effective promotion of human happiness. So far as we are concerned, this is a human world: therefore the two things that really matter are the contentment of the individual human body, and the enlargement of the individual human soul, spirit, or call it what you like.

PRACTICAL MAN. I see so many gaps in your argument.

LINKLATER. So do I. But for the moment I am more interested in the argument than the gaps.

PRACTICAL MAN. I smell a kind of noble priggery in your words. I had not suspected you of this. But now I remember that all comedians desire to play a tragic part, and Hamlet for ever hides beneath

a clown's white paint. It was Keats, I think, who wrote:
> 'None shall usurp that height
> Save those to whom the miseries of the world
> Are misery, and will not let them rest.'

Is it now your ambition to compete for a place on that eminence?

LINKLATER (*furiously*). Will you kindly go to hell and stay there?

PRACTICAL MAN. A rivederci!

I find it very hard to argue a good case. To defend an impossible thesis or support the patently ridiculous is easy and amusing, but to speak for what I truly feel to be good, and greatly good, is confoundedly difficult. On the one side is the Scylla of sentimental overstatement, on the other the Charybdis of platitude: and between them the breeze may fail, the current may fail, and one's vessel lie becalmed. There are happy people, I know, whose speech comes freely from intestinal depths. But I am not of these. My brain is fairly communicative, but my guts are analphabetic. There are times when I do wear my heart on my sleeve, but even then—such are the difficulties of its passage from the sternal cavity—it wears a strange unlikely look, and is not often recognized. It is, indeed, generally taken for a lemon.

PRELUDE IN THE FIRST PERSON SINGULAR

But for this matter of England, the proem, I think, is tuned. I have refrained from pulling out all the stops. I have not risen skyward on the seat of the Mighty Wurlitzer. *Vox humana* has been heard for no more than a bar or two. It will be a quiet performance.

II
ROUNDABOUT AND SWINGS

II
ROUNDABOUT AND SWINGS

ACCORDING to Sir Walter Scott, three hundred and fourteen battles were fought between England and Scotland prior to the Union of 1707. I have not checked the figure, but it would probably be more accurate to say that so many battles had occurred between Englishmen and Scots: not all those conflicts were affairs of political importance: many were expressions of sectional or individual feeling, and some of them, frankly fought for loot, were happily productive of a ballad. They were battles of that apparently reasonable kind which, for so long, preserved the good name of war.

Engagements of that kind must be distinguished from the *ex officio* battles that more bloodily and less profitably punctuated the historic struggle between England and Scotland. In this long warfare, Scotland was the first aggressor. The union of the Picts and Scots under Kenneth MacAlpine gave to part of

Scotland something in the nature of a national entity, and for two hundred years Albyn, that embryonic Scotland, fought to detach the Lothians from the kingdom of Northumbria. In 1018 Malcolm II defeated the Northumbrians at Carham, and Scotland marched southwards to the Tweed. The Celtic kingdom extended its boundaries and enclosed that which would in time destroy its Celtic character: in the Lothians the English language and the English law prevailed.

The great-grandson of Malcolm II was Malcolm Canmore, who, after some years of exile in the court of Edward the Confessor, fought his way to the Scottish throne, and in 1068 or thereabout married Margaret, sister of Edgar the Atheling, then with her brother a refugee in Scotland from the wrath of William the Conqueror. Malcolm, a vigorous and accomplished soldier, was much under the influence of his English wife. She was one of those strong, interfering, pious and persistent women of whom England has successfully bred a considerable number. The rigours and prohibitions of the Sabbath day, which in more recent centuries became a Scottish tradition, were introduced to Scotland by her. She objected to the Gaelic Mass, and summoned English clergy to celebrate it in Latin. She gave English names to her sons, she sheltered the English fugitives who sought safety from William's conquest, she was a civilizing influence. She rebuilt the monastery of Iona, and her son David remade the whole kingdom. It was Margaret who brought Scotland out of the Dark Ages into the armour-glinting light of Mediævalism. If she did this at the expense of the Celtic ethos, it was because the Celtic ethos was barbaric, and she destroyed nothing that was not self-doomed to destruction. The effect of her reign, and of her sons' reigning, was to bring Scotland into closer competition with England; but had it not been for them Scotland might never again have had the strength to compete. Celtic Scotland might have become what Celtic Ireland became. Margaret and her sons saved it from that tragic fate, as Sigurd, Earl of Orkney, might have saved Ireland, had the disastrous battle of Clontarf gone the other way.

It was Edgar, Margaret's second son, who first removed the royal court from Dunfermline to Edinburgh; and David, her fourth son, acquiring by marriage the Honour of Huntingdon and the Earldom of Northampton, became in respect of those titles an English baron. Here were the seeds of greatness and disaster: to be a strategic capital, Edinburgh was too near the frontier; and English baronies in the hands of Scottish kings, profitable though they doubtless were, gave English kings a partial claim to overlordship. For centuries this claim was a characteristic feature of Anglo-Scottish relations; and Scottish kings, acknowledging it as often as they were compelled to, repudiated it with a like regularity. The oath of allegiance and the acknowledgment that such-and-such a monarch was William's man or Edward's man, were a political convention of the times, promoting gratification on the one side, and giving breathing-space to the other. The English kings who exacted such a pledge were possibly optimistic about its fulfilment; the Scottish kings had no such illusion. The English kings, dynastically ambitious, hoped for the addition of Scotland to their titles; the Scottish kings, more concerned with acres than honour, persisted in trying to extend their boundaries to the Tees.

The greatest of Margaret's sons was David, whose character was a blend of paternal and maternal qualities. He was warlike and pious, he was fervid and practical. Under his energetic rule Scotland became progressively organized, feudalized, Anglicized and urbanized. These changes, of course, were largely though not entirely confined to the south. Highland society, naturally recoiling, found means of self-preservation in the clan system. David built great abbeys, enriched the clergy, and making the Church of Rome the national church, gave Scotland a core of sturdy and consistent patriotism. He was succeeded by Malcolm the Maiden, William the Lyon, and the two Alexanders, whose policy, with intermissions and varying success, was consolidation of the system established by David. Scotland took its place in the comity of Europe, and the glowing light that lit then the churches and the schools and the markets of Europe, visited also for a little time our northern skies; so that in a later age, out of the squalor and brutality and thin-sided heroism of long warfare, men looked back with yearning to this Golden Age.

Loudly through the land had risen the noise of the builders, while the abbeys and great churches grew among the trees and opened their long windows and their round windows to the smooth round hills. Loudly in the sea-ports had risen the voices of the foreign sailors as the trading-ships came in from England and from Italy, from Flanders and the Baltic.

Loudly—or perhaps quietly—sang the harvesters, for serfdom had been abolished and men in the fields worked free; and loudly disputed the wandering scholars of Scotland in Oxford and Paris and Bologna. But when the century grew old there came other noises to drown this cheerful clamour, and the King's death and the end of happiness were foretold by thunder out of season; and to the music of roaring surf the Maid of Norway died.

Now English influence had been paramount in bringing those happy times to Scotland. It was the Saxon princess Margaret who opened the door to them. It was her sons and descendants, their Anglo-Norman friends and servants, who brought the new knowledge and the new ideas on which the new order was founded. Nor was this the whole sum of England's beneficence, for during much of the Twelfth Century her king and nobles were so much engaged by civil strife and the extravagant foreign policy of Henry III that they had no time to interfere with Scotland. Civil war in England was for centuries God's greatest gift to her poor relation: as Edward I was one of His several curses.

To the English historian Edward's earnest rapacity and vindictive ambition—it became like a malignant growth in him—may be to some extent condoned by his land laws, his defiance of the Pope, and his domestic virtues. But to the Scot and the Welshman he is simply a figure of destruction. Taking a bailiff's advantage of the situation in Scotland—the Maid of Norway's death had left an empty throne and a chorus of claimants—he exacted oaths of allegiance from the dozen postulants, selected John Balliol as King, and by a policy of calculated insult and oppression made life so intolerable for him that rebellion was inevitable. Thereupon Edward, unmasking his intention, invaded Scotland and christened a new era of hatred in the bloody sack of Berwick. Balliol's rebellion was stamped out; and the long war began.

This is no place to write of Falkirk and Bannockburn, of Wallace and the Bruce. There had been battles before Falkirk and gallantry before Wallace: though never such gallantry. But neither had there been such hatred as came now. Hatred was of Edward's making. When Alexander died, Scotland was a land at peace, a land of busy and various interests, happy in its prosperity, and eager for culture. When Edward died it was poor and bloody and desperate, a land with one determination, to live in despite of England, and with one luxury, hatred of England. It was in the poor people and the small people that hatred first became self-conscious. It was the common people of Scotland who fought beside Wallace, himself a poor knight's son, and saved Scotland alive. Like a babe in the womb, waking now and moving, patriotism took possession of the common body of Scotland. So much may be granted to the English king, that he made all Scotland acutely conscious of its nationhood.

But the tragedy of that quickening is already apparent: in one sentence I have called the birth hatred, in the next it is patriotism: for under Edward's hammer they were synonymous. The psychological effect of that ambiguity or confusion of principles has been enormous. In the unhappiness of Scotland's subsequent history there is apparent a certain deformity of the national character, which—I do not think it fanciful to say—took its origin from that primary distortion. To love one's own country is natural and pleasant and proper; but when that natural love is born in the shape and similitude of hatred, then nature must be deformed, and it is only necessary to consider the two salient features of Scotland's later history to see that deformity in action: Presbytery and the Industrial Revolution were both characterized by brutal excess, by mortification of the flesh, and starvation of the spirit. At the hands of the Industrialists and the Kirk Sessions Scotland wilfully mutilated itself. Hatred, so long nourished by the English wars, turned inwards and maimed its own body. Compelled by necessity to live violently, violence became a Scottish characteristic; and the habit of patriotic homicide, degenerating after centuries' use, very nearly became suicide. The Kirk, fearing or hating beauty and the zest of humankind, turned its face to a dreary and a sterile heaven of its own invention; the Industrialists set their feet on humankind and trod it down in the obscene squalor of the slums. *Edwardus primus Scottorum malleus hic est.*

The War of Independence, begun by Wallace in 1297, came to an end in 1328, with Scotland triumphant and hopelessly impoverished. Berwick, the richest town in the country, had become a permanent battlefield. Vast areas of land had gone out of cultivation, trade was ruined, and useful citizens had become soldiers.

In 1332 another war began, Scotland was reconquered, and again fought its way to freedom.

ROUNDABOUT AND SWINGS

In 1346, recklessly invading England to show their love for France, the Scots were utterly defeated at Neville's Cross. Four years later they attacked Carlisle, and by infection from its garrison brought home the Black Death. As a result of this distemper, a third of Scotland's population died. In 1356 Edward III crossed the border and celebrated his Burnt Candelmas by destroying the Lamp of Lothian and every town and village between Berwick and Edinburgh. David II, a prisoner in England, was released on promise of a ransom of a hundred thousand marks; but the money could not be paid.

For some years there was comparative peace—except for civil war and strife on the Border—but in 1381, to oblige a party of thirty French gentlemen seeking adventure, a Scottish force invaded Northumberland and took a deal of booty; in the following spring the Earls of Northumberland and Nottingham, by way of reprisal, devastated the Lothians, demolished Edinburgh, and burnt Haddington. Three years later, repaying another Scots invasion, Richard II burnt Melrose Abbey, Edinburgh, Perth, and Dundee. The Scots took their revenge at Otterbourne, a more profitable affray than most, for it gave us the excellent ballad of Chevy Chase. . . .

But I grow tired of this bloody recital, this wretched tale of hatred whose author was Edward I. And not only the English wars were of his begetting. Civil strife in Scotland, of which there was plenty, was also due to him in so far as the great houses that fomented it had become great by their participation in the War of Independence; in so far as he had turned Scotland into a nation of truculent soldiers; and in so far as poverty, which was of his making, could make men readier for war because they had so little to lose by war. That England broke the back of Scotland's early history can hardly be disputed. From 1068, or thereby, when Malcolm married his Saxon princess, to 1292, when the third Alexander died, was a period of development: the Fourteenth Century, despite the Bruce's victorious campaign, was a period of decay.

But in the Fifteenth Century Scotland's fortunes began to mend, and this, in a negative way, was also due to England: for England was too busy with the remaining decades of the Hundred Years' War and the Wars of the Roses to think much about her Northern neighbour.—England also suffered for having turned so many honest yeomen into soldiers.—This reaction of Scotland culminated in the hazardous brilliance of James IV's inspiring reign. A little fine weather out of that high summer which is called the Renaissance was lent to Scotland, and wealth consorted with culture in an equal growth. It was the age of Dunbar and Gavin Douglas and Henryson. The King built a navy and encouraged the art of printing. Trade grew rapidly. Between 1414 and 1498 the Universities of St Andrews, Glasgow, and Aberdeen were founded; and the Education Act of 1496 envisaged a scholar and a lawyer in the house of every baron and freeholder in the kingdom. On the testimony of Ayala, the Spanish Ambassador, the towns and villages were populous. The houses, well built of stone, had glass windows, many chimneys, and all the furniture that might be found in Italy and Spain and France. The people were frankly ostentatious in their new wealth, and the women—honest, courteous, and bold—dressed more handsomely than those of England.

Riches and ostentation, a relish for life and a bold demeanour, love of learning and a great skill in poetry—the Renaissance had come indeed to Scotland, but its works were built on treacherous foundations. Under a thin surface of new soil still lay the old habit of violence, the traditional hostility to England, and our spendthrift love for France. Henry VIII went to war with France: the Queen of France besought King James, with a ring from her own finger, to advance three feet into English ground and strike a blow for her honour: James, and a great army with him, willing enough for such a venture, went three feet too far.

The English strategy was daring, their tactics sufficient, their weapons superior, their behaviour worthy of all praise. At Flodden they won a great and well-deserved victory. But for Scotland Flodden was like a shipwreck in which all the officers and first-class passengers were drowned. Flodden cried halt to the advancing renaissance, and Dunbar's nightmare chorus, *Timor mortis conturbat me*, appeared to have been plain revelation. Scotland now entered as miserable a period of existence as it had ever known. France continually thrust it into war with England, to which indeed its congenital disposition inclined it, and Henry VIII discovered an imperialistic ambition as resolute and almost as ruthless as Edward I's. Deciding to acquire Scotland as a marriage portion for his son's wife, he temporarily betrothed the infant Edward to the nursling Mary, and suborned a willing party of Scots nobles to support his project. Scotland, already bloodily divided by the contestant greed of the Douglases and the Hamiltons, was further bewildered by English spies and English agents. And when the traditional Francophile policy prevailed, Henry sent punitive expeditions to harden all hearts with fire and sword. The Earl of Hertford's three incursions did irreparable damage. Corn could grow again, and cattle be bred again; towns and villages might be built again, and children grow into soldiers as tall as those who were killed; but Hertford laid in ruin the abbeys of Kelso, Dryburgh, Roxburgh, Coldingham and Melrose—it had been restored since Richard II's visit—and now there was neither ability nor the will to build again in this fashion. And in the battles of Pinkie and Solway Moss Scotland was not only defeated but disgraced. The Renaissance had a bitter aftermath.

But now the situation grows more complicated. Now the Church was also at war. In 1517 Luther had hoisted the rebel flag at Wittenberg, and in 1535 Henry VIII, banishing the Pope from his dominions, had enriched himself with the enormous wealth of the Church in England. In Scotland the Church was fantastically wealthy and deplorably corrupt. Men of good feeling took the example of Luther, and good business-men followed Henry's lead. They found common cause in a common enmity, and built a new religion on the same foundations as had served for Scottish patriotism. Hatred, that is. Hatred of England had kept Scotland at war for rather more than two hundred years, and now, for too long, hatred of Rome was to engage it in other wars. Patriotism founded on hatred, by breeding a habit of violence, had promoted internal dissension whenever a cessation of foreign hostility had given Scotland time to be self-conscious. Religion, grown on greed and hatred, promoted bitterness, intolerance, and envy. It may be said, without possibility of contradiction, that Scotland had been forced into its conception of patriotism-as-hatred by the destructive policy of Edward I. It may also be said, without much fear of denial, that Scotland was initially led to confuse religion with hatred and jealousy by the wealth and corruption of the Roman Church in Scotland. But despite compulsion on the one hand, and strong provocation on the other, it is none the less regrettable that our love of country and love of God should both have been expressed by hatred of our fellow-men. It must be noted, however, that the Reformers did not hate England: they hated France instead, which was the fist of Rome. Under the regency of Mary of Lorraine Scotland nearly became a French province, and the New Party, reacting against the threat of French domination, and much impressed by Henry VIII's remunerative clerical policy, became markedly Anglophile.

III

THE KIRK OF SCOTLAND

III

THE KIRK OF SCOTLAND

THE history of the Kirk of Scotland is strictly relevant to a consideration of English influence on Scotland, for international politics played a dominant part in its development, and it was indebted to England for its establishment and re-establishment, for much of its dissension and most of its ritual.

Consider on the one hand the excessive wealth, the widespread incompetence, and the serious corruption of the Roman Church in Scotland: and assume, in reaction to the incompetence and corruption, a growing desire for a new demonstration of the validity of the spiritual life. Put on the same side fear of France's growing political ascendancy in Scotland, and remember the identification of French and Papal interests. There you have the composite rock out of which the stream was to flow. Now on the other hand put Luther, who had proclaimed rebellion in Germany; Henry VIII, who had demonstrated the vincibility of the Pope in England; and Calvin, who had formulated a creed admirably suited for demagogy. There you have preceptors for the young Moses; and having learnt his lesson, John Knox returned to Scotland and smote upon the rock.

In 1557 the Lords of the self-styled Congregation of Christ, with one eye on the Church's enormous wealth, bound themselves never to rest till they had made their newly adopted faith the national religion. Two years later, after listening to a sermon by Knox, the Reformers began their destruction of the monasteries. Open war followed between the Congregation and the Regent, Mary of Lorraine, who had imported a considerable body of French troops. The rebels were supported by England: Elizabeth sent them £3000, a fleet to blockade the Forth, and later an army. The French, after negotiation, retired to France, and the Protestants were triumphant. Knox and his fellow-ministers formulated a Confession of Faith which the Estates approved by an overwhelming majority. Three Acts were passed: abolishing the jurisdiction of the Pope, condemning all doctrine and practice contrary to the new creed, and forbidding he celebration of the Mass in Scotland. In 1561, the first Book of Discipline—a code of belief and behaviour for the whole nation—caused a division of opinion in the Congregation on the question of the disposal of the Church's property, much of which had already been acquired by the nobles. The Reformers found their most numerous support among the recently risen middle class, whose resentment against the wastefulness, rapacity, and profligacy of the old Church was natural and sincere.

Shortly after the appearance of the Book of Discipline, Mary, Queen of Scots, came home, and by wise and tolerant rule maintained peace in the Kingdom for four years, despite the ceaseless provocation and incitement to violence of Knox and his fellow-ministers. She confirmed by proclamation the legality of the new religious settlement, and her prudence encouraged more moderate views in the General Assembly. Her flight to England, however, was followed by civil war. The problem of the disposal of Church property re-appeared, and in opposition to the Protestant ministers, who claimed to be the rightful legatees, the Earl of Morton, then or soon to be Regent, maintained that the Sovereign alone could settle that question. Morton, looking forward to the Union of the Crowns, believed that union of the English and Scots churches would also be desirable. At his instance a Convention decided to preserve the titles of Archbishop, Bishop, Abbot, and Prior, which had been abolished by the Book of Discipline. A year or two later, in the General Assembly, Melville raised the question whether Episcopacy had the authority of Scripture, and Scotland's main interest for the next hundred years was defined. The civil war continued.

In Scotland there was continual dread of a Roman restoration, led by Philip of Spain. This may explain, in some part, the tyranny of ecclesiastical rule, and the excessive and growing claims to secular authority made by the ministers. Pulpits were regularly used for propaganda, and the Assembly employed its power of excommunication as a political instrument. In 1580, at Dundee, Episcopacy was condemned, and in the following year the Assembly established the Presbyteries and sanctioned the Second Book of Discipline, which postulated jurisdiction independent of the State. By 1584 James VI, an extraordinarily able king, had made his position sufficiently strong to support a declaration that he, and he only, being head of the Church as well as of the State, could appoint bishops and sanction meetings of the General Assembly. He forbade pulpit-criticism of public affairs; and commanded ministers to subscribe to his postulates. The leading ministers sought refuge in England. In 1586, after the conclusion of a defensive and offensive alliance between England and Scotland, the ministers returned. But the Kirk was now divided, and when James removed to the throne of England he could say that Presbytery was finished. He maintained the liveliest interest in Scottish affairs, and for the next decade he was busy with the establishment of diocesan episcopacy. The Scottish nobility, whom James's predecessors had found so troublesome, gave no trouble during this period: their complacence was bought with judicious parcels of the old Church's property.

Having established episcopacy, James persuaded an Assembly at Perth, in 1618, to approve the practice of kneeling for Communion, the private administration of Communion and Baptism in case of necessity, the observance of Christian festivals, and confirmation by Bishops. These five articles, especially the first, roused much opposition, and despite pressure the majority of communicants remained seated. All parties, however, agreed on one point: that detestation of Popery was the most convincing sign of orthodoxy.

Charles I, soon after his accession, passed an Act of Revocation, annexing for the public weal all Church and Crown lands alienated since 1542. This ill-advised measure, by depriving the nobles of the wealth that had made them Episcopalians, turned them into Presbyterians again, and paved the road to the great rebellion. By reorganization of the system of teinds, Charles secured to ministers a permanent and sufficient income, but the beneficence was ill timed: reforms, unless very gradually effected, invariably arouse indignation. In 1637, during a total eclipse of reason, the King endeavoured to replace Knox's service-book—the Book of Common Order—with what was known as Laud's Liturgy. A triple smell of Popery, English domination, and royal absolutism rose from this unfortunate book, and its introduction was marked by a lively riot in St Giles. In spite of a national ' Supplication ' Charles refused to recall it, and the answer to his obstinacy was the National League and Covenant. This was based on the Negative Confession of Faith, authorized by James VI in 1581, condemning the tenets of the Roman Church: it enumerated the various Acts of Confirmation of this Confession; it noted the inconsistency of Charles's policy with these Acts; it affirmed the intention of its signatories to defend jointly the Crown and True Religion. The only important town which refused to sign the Covenant was Aberdeen.

A General Assembly, sitting without royal authority, abolished the episcopal order, and the breakdown of subsequent negotiations was followed by the First Bishops' War. The English temper, now strongly inclined to Puritanism, prevented Charles from taking the field in any great strength. The Covenanters, after a series of small successes against Episcopalians in the north-east of Scotland, faced the Royal army near Berwick. There was no fighting; and the subsequent pacification of Berwick was inconclusive. Two months later the Covenanters showed themselves as unreasonable as Charles had been: an Act was passed compelling the whole nation to subscribe the Covenant. Having refuted the absolutism of the Czar, that is, the Soviet declared itself absolute. The English Parliament—the Short Parliament—whose sympathy was with the Covenanters, refused to grant supplies for a Scottish war, and Charles was unable to oppose Leslie's well-disciplined army when it crossed the Border to present its demands. Charles was no longer master of either of his kingdoms. The Covenanting Army remained in England for a year, well paid by the Long Parliament, and at the service of the English Puritans if need should arise.

Charles now came to Scotland, prepared to ratify the Acts against Episcopacy, and hoping to find a party with which to oppose the English Parliament: for now, with Stafford dead and Laud in prison, Scotland seemed to him less hostile than England. There appeared, at least, to be more division of opinion there. He yielded to the Scottish Parliament his previously asserted prerogative of nominating Privy Councillors and other officers of State, and returned to England without any access of strength.

The war between Charles and his Parliament began in 1642. Scotland, with its excellent army, was in a position to decide the issue, and Cavaliers and Roundheads equally desired and appealed for its support. After considerable opposition a Convention of Estates decided to accept a formal proposal of alliance by the English Parliament. The General Assembly, concurring with the decision, put forward as the treaty of alliance the Solemn League and Covenant, the principal item on whose programme was the reformation of religion in Britain 'according to the Word of God.' Though civil liberty was of more interest to the English, they badly needed assistance, and the

Covenant, slightly modified, was accepted. Thereupon a Scottish army, under that capable soldier Leslie, crossed the Border and remained in England for three years. It was instrumental in holding the northern counties for Parliament, and at first it was very well paid for this decisive service.

Meanwhile Montrose had raised a Royalist army in Scotland—a useful contingent of which was Irish—and for a year he demonstrated the art of war with such daring felicity that even the most ardent lovers of peace must yield him adulterous admiration. He was at last defeated by David Leslie, a nephew of the older General, and his magnificent campaign had the unfortunate effect of increasing the cruelty and bitterness of Scotland's internecine warfare.

The Covenanters were now bitterly disappointed by events in England. They had hoped, with their army, to impose on both countries government by a Presbyterian soviet. But Cromwell's Independents preferred a more individual interpretation of life and scripture, and as Cromwell no longer needed the Scots—Charles's defeat at Naseby had killed the Royalist cause—their supplies were cut off and they were variously encouraged to go home. Their problem was simplified in May, 1646, when Charles surrendered himself to them at Newark. The Scots retired to Newcastle and began negotiations. They had two objects in view: to persuade Charles to subscribe the Covenant, and to extract from England their arrears of pay. England paid; but Charles refused his subscription. The Covenanters, declining to keep a king who would not obey them, handed him over to England. It is unfair to say that they sold him. They merely wrote off a liability in return for new stock.

In addition to a promise of £400,000, the Covenanters brought home the Longer and Shorter Catechisms, a metrical version of the Psalms, and a Confession of Faith: these being the lucubrations of the Westminster Assembly of Divines. Of these importations the Shorter Catechism alone was to cause more and more prolonged suffering than any other of England's punitive incursions.

The situation in Scotland now changed. Their estates being no longer threatened by the Act of Revocation, the nobles regained their loyalty to the King, and desired the English Parliament to release him and forthwith establish the Presbyterian system in England in accordance with the Solemn League and Covenant. The ministers strenuously opposed the plan to bring Charles to Scotland, but a poorly equipped army was despatched to enforce these demands; and was cut to pieces by Cromwell. In October, 1647, Cromwell came to Edinburgh, and a defensive alliance against all forms of Malignancy was made between the anti-Royalist Covenanters and the English Independents. It did not last long. Fifteen months later Charles was executed, and the Scottish Estates, in open defiance of England, proclaimed his son King of Great Britain, France, and Ireland. It had been Charles's misfortune to live in an age when the Divine Right of Kings conflicted with the Covenanters' monopoly of God. But the Covenanters still believed that monarchy—obedient monarchy—was the natural form of government, and their proclamation of Charles II was an indignant rebuff to the regicides.

Charles II came to Scotland—he had been living at the Hague—and signed the Covenants. A month later he was followed by Cromwell, with an army. Scotland was hopelessly divided, but a fair-sized force was mobilized, and the command given to David Leslie. Leslie's generalship was too much for Cromwell, who was driven into an awkward corner at Dunbar. But the Kirk was too much for Leslie. The ministers insisted on purging his army of all taint of malignancy—which meant discharging his most useful soldiers—and then, at Dunbar, ordered the godly remnant downhill to an appalling defeat.

The situation changed again. The Covenanters divided into a Left Wing called the Remonstrants, who disowned their new king; and a Right Wing, the Resolutioners, who opened their ranks to friendly Malignants, and got Charles crowned at Scone. Cromwell, in the meantime, had made his occupation of southern Scotland fairly secure. But an army of the Right Wing, under Leslie, suddenly and daringly invaded England; where it found no support from English Royalists, and was defeated at Worcester.

For nine years Scotland was occupied by Cromwell's garrisons and governed by English commissioners. The English campaign, with a massacre at Dundee to help it, had been bloody and successful. The English government was good, though too costly. The ministers, still divided into Resolutioners and Remonstrants, were discouraged from preaching politics, and sympathetic observers detected a revival of religious interest. Cromwell established a temporary union of the two countries, and Scotland sent thirty members —mostly English officials—to the Commonwealth

Parliament. Scotland gained free trade with England and its colonies, but by trade regulations in the interests of England lost its export markets for hides and wool. Ratification of the Act of Union was prevented by Presbyterian lobbying, because provision had been made for freedom of conscience, which the northern monopolists of God refused to tolerate.

The fall of the Long Parliament and the restoration of Charles II in 1660 gave Scotland a parliament of its own again. It was known as the Drunken Parliament. It passed three hundred and ninety-three Acts in six months, including a Rescissory Act which nullified all parliamentary proceedings of the last twenty-seven years. The principle of absolute monarchy was re-asserted, and unhappily for the Kirk Charles II believed that Presbytery was no religion for a gentleman.

It was a very much modified form of Episcopacy that Charles re-imposed on Scotland. Neither prayer-book nor surplice were introduced. The Presbyteries remained, but bishops were appointed to control them; and lay patronage was restored. It was a political episcopacy, and Scotland would probably have submitted to it without any great complaint had it not been for the criminal folly of those then ruling

THE KIRK OF SCOTLAND

Scotland. Two or three hundred ministers resigned their charges rather than accept the new order, and were replaced by a hastily recruited and illiterate pastorate, whose sermons were so little to the taste of a theological people that their churches were deserted, and the congregations worshipped under their own ejected ministers in the open air. Instead of leaving these robust seceders to the inevitable attrition of northern weather, Charles's government in Scotland was so incredibly impolitic as to flatter them with persecution. That wretched tale began of conventicles in the heather, and dragoons casting widely, like hounds on the trail of a stubborn fox, for the rebellious noise of a psalm. The south-west of Scotland was the home of pious obduracy. Persecution begat heroism, heroism became fanaticism, and fanaticism provoked a bloodier persecution. There were two or three small scrambling battles between royal troops and Covenanters so inexpugnably quarrelsome that their ever-present ministers would preach more hotly against each other than against the attacking enemy. The unconquerable rump of the Covenants was the desperate sect of *exaltés* called Cameronians. They defied Bishop and Presbyter alike. In ridiculous solemnity they pronounced Charles and his ministers excommunicate. They were hunted on the hills like partridges, they were caught and executed or sent to the Barbadoes, and they were never quite defeated.

But Presbytery was defeated, partly by terrorization, and partly by the Acts of Indulgence, that re-admitted recalcitrant ministers who would accept the episcopalian supremacy of the Crown. If Charles's successor had been like Charles, a Protestant, Presbytery in Scotland might have vanished—in name, if not in form—for ever. But James VII and II was a stubborn Catholic. Stubborn as a Cameronian.—A plague on both their houses? It is the just comment on religion in Scotland.—James packed his Council with Catholics, suspended all laws against Catholics, and brought back to Edinburgh what the Covenant had forcefully called 'the devilish mass and the blasphemous priesthood.' The Roman bogey, thus raised again, frightened even Royalists into inaction when the revolution in England evicted James and gave his throne to the cold unhealthy Dutchman. William, the new king, did no good to Scotland, though he restored Presbytery and abandoned religious persecution when he found it unprofitable.—Two hundred Episcopalian ministers were removed because they would not pray for him.—From this time the Kirk was immune from external attack, though five years after the Union of the Parliaments it was seriously offended by an Act of Toleration, to protect the Episcopal Church, and by the restoration of lay patronage, in violation of the Act of Security. But though its existence was no longer threatened from without, its later happiness was to be disturbed from within, by a certain fissiparity that became one of its more notable characteristics. For some considerable time after the Revolution of 1689, however, economic affairs rather than theological occupied the attention of Scotland; and during much of the Eighteenth Century there was a growing fear that religion might degenerate into mere morality.

For a time, indeed, under the influence of Hume, educated opinion in Scotland became remarkably free-thinking: in 1766 Professor Gregory, writing to Beattie, could say that 'absolute dogmatic atheism' was the present tone in Edinburgh. But that was a rhetorical statement. Under the Moderate Party, however, the Kirk, in defiance of Calvin, did become tolerant for the first time in its history. It also suffered, in 1746, what is generally called its first secession, though the Cameronian Societies had long since left it, and re-christened themselves the Reformed Presbyterians. The Original Seceders (of 1746) divided from the parent body on the old question of patronage. Later, disputing the interpretation of an oath 'to profess and allow the true religion presently professed,' the Seceders split into Burghers and Anti-Burghers. Holding different opinions about the proper conduct of the Communion Service, the Anti-Burghers then broke up into Lifters and Anti-Lifters. A vital dispute on the power of the civil authority to exact obedience in religious matters then divided Burghers, Lifters, and Anti-Lifters into Auld Lichts and New Lichts and the several combinations made possible by this latest fission.

In the parent body the Moderate Party became the New Moderates, and were opposed by the Highflyers, who later became the popular Evangelical Party. The New Moderates suffered another secession—patronage was again in conflict with the congregation's demand to choose their own ministers—and the Relief Church was formed. Moderatism declined when zeal, made fashionable by the French Revolution, began to dispossess the cool speculative temper of the Eighteenth Century; and the Evangelicals became the dominant party. In 1843, built once more on the old quarrel with patronage, the Free Church was founded. This was the last of the great secessions.

THE KIRK OF SCOTLAND

Centrifugal force had now spent itself; the passion for divergence died; and slowly the scattered parts acknowledge centripetal leanings. Coalition became the prevailing temper of the times, and the Kirk obeyed it. In 1929 the Church of Scotland, save a stubborn small minority, was re-united.

But this must be remembered, that despite a great number of superficial differences the foundation of the Kirk remained whole and unaltered. And this foundation was the solid rock—or concrete rather, for it was artificial—of the Westminster Confession of Faith, with its reinforcement of the two Catechisms. This was the system, says Hume Brown, that made Scotland 'a nation of theologians: all came from the Westminster Assembly, and produced that astonishing precision of thought regarding the mysteries of human destiny which has ever since been one of the national characteristics.' That is no uncommon view. It is, indeed—or was a generation ago—the general opinion held in Scotland. Every Scot prided himself on 'astonishing precision of thought,' and the majority were ready to ascribe this notable faculty to their training in that strikingly un-English importation from England, the Shorter Catechism.

What England has meant to Scotland. . . . Queen

Margaret and civilization; Edward I and ages of hatred; Chaucer to a few; the Auld Alliance with France; the establishment of the Reformation; peace under Cromwell; the defeat at Darien; military service and high command in the great armies of England; freedom to live and to trade overseas; opportunities of wealth; a slow emasculation; a share in Britannic power and prestige; the invasion of English standards of politeness; the culture, and physical culture, of the English public schools; and the Shorter Catechism.

The Catechism consists of a hundred and seven questions and the same number of answers. It was approved by a General Assembly, sitting in Edinburgh in 1648, as an instrument of uniformity in the Kirk, and appointed 'to be a directory for catechizing such as are of weaker capacity.' Generation after generation of children was compelled to learn the Catechism by heart. It was not a cheerful view of life that it presented:

QUESTION 16. *Did all mankind fall in Adam's first transgression?*
ANSWER. The covenant being made with Adam, not only for himself, but for his posterity; all mankind, descending from him by ordinary generation, sinned in him, and fell with him, in his first transgression.

QUESTION 17. *Into what estate did the fall bring mankind?*

ANSWER. The fall brought mankind into an estate of sin and misery.

QUESTION 18. *Wherein consists the sinfulness of that estate whereinto man fell?*

ANSWER. The sinfulness of that estate whereinto man fell, consists in the guilt of Adam's first sin, the want of original righteousness, and the corruption of his whole nature, which is commonly called Original Sin, together with all actual transgressions which proceed from it.

QUESTION 19. *What is the misery of that estate whereinto man fell?*

ANSWER. All mankind by their fall lost Communion with God, are under His wrath and curse, and so made liable to all miseries in this life, to death itself, and to the pains of hell for ever.

Perhaps these answers were indeed such as to inculcate an 'astonishing precision of thought regarding the mysteries of human destiny'; but it is a precision that most of us would gladly be without. And such immoderate concern with the ultimate mysteries of human destiny was perhaps responsible for the ministers' strange neglect of immediate phenomena almost as mysterious as the predestined damnation in which they believed.

In the Eighteenth and Nineteenth Centuries, tens

THE KIRK OF SCOTLAND

of thousands of Highland crofters, to make room for sheep, were evicted from land that was theirs by the title of immemorial usage. In the Nineteenth Century, tens of thousands of men, women, and children were compelled, by the iron laws of Industrial Revolution, to live in such filth and misery and squalor as sicken the imagination. Many of the ministers facilitated the evictions by telling the crofters that this calamity was punishment for their wickedness. The ministers of the Kirk that had for so long claimed jurisdiction in secular as well as in spiritual matters, watched without any effective protest the degradation of the people under the Moloch of Industrialism. The Kirk that had defied the Pope of Rome, the Kings of England and France and Scotland, offered no effectual resistance to the Highland landlords and southern industrialists who banished or debased its pitifully faithful congregations.

Why was the Kirk, with its 'astonishing precision of thought,' so supine in these crises? Because of its solitary concern with the soul of man? But it had often enough interfered with the bodies of men by preventing them from dancing, drinking, and walking abroad on the Sabbath day. Because its battles for existence had exhausted it? Because its long struggle had always been a selfish struggle, a struggle for its own dominion, for its rents, and its monopoly of salvation? Because its birth had been hatred of Rome, its youth had been hatred of Episcopacy, and now in its maturity there was no room for charity? Because of the verse from Timothy with which it buttressed the answer to the seventy-fourth question in the Catechism: 'If any provide not for his own, and specially for those of his own house, he hath denied the faith, and is worse than an infidel'? For by a large interpretation of this text the poor men of Sutherland and the poor men of the slums, being guilty of poverty and having failed to provide for their own, were worse than infidels, and so beyond the interest or the care of the Kirk. The Kirk was now somewhat prone to confuse prosperity with virtue: an identification it ingeniously strengthened by the example of Joseph, who had virtuously 'gathered up all the money that was found in the land of Egypt.'

But the Kirk performed its duty according to its lights: it taught children the meaning of Effectual Calling and the difference between Justification, Adoption, and Sanctification. It taught their elders that among the sins forbidden by the Seventh Com-

THE KIRK OF SCOTLAND

mandment—co-partners in evil with rape, incest, and sodomy—were 'books, pictures, dancings, and stage-playing.' And for the system on which this teaching depended—surely the most un-English thing that ever crossed the Border—the Kirk was indebted to England. It was, moreover, rewarded for what seems to us a gloomy, sterile, and unnatural doctrine with Scotland's true and enduring affection.

Why was the Kirk, with its harsh teaching, so richly rewarded with trust and love? Obviously because it gave Scotland what Scotland wanted. And why did Scotland want a creed so hostile to pleasure? Because 'he that loveth pleasure shall be a poor man, he that loveth wine and oil shall not be rich'; and Scotland, having been poor for so long, had come to a feverish desire for riches. And because Scotland had lived in the midst of so many perils its God must be a jealous God, such a God as the war-like and peril-girt tribes of Israel had found serviceable; Egypt and Assyria were not otherwise than England and Rome, Edward I had played Pharaoh to the Scots, and Ashtaroth was like a Popish idol; the God of David had taught David to throw stones. For a people who had suffered too much, from too many foes, there was great comfort in a creed so lavish in damnation.

IV

THE DARK AGES

IV
THE DARK AGES

'But if in the Highlands the people were trying to exist upon a diet of boiled grass and nettles, the case was even worse in the city wynds. Within a circle of twelve miles of Glasgow there were ten thousand paupers receiving on an average not more than one shilling and sixpence a week. . . . The child serfs in West of Scotland bleachfields were being worked from eleven to eighteen hours daily in stoves heated from eighty to a hundred degrees; at Pollokshaws children were occasionally worked two and three days and nights consecutively. . . . The Whig Act of 1851 regulating magisterial punishment of young children allowed a sentence of thirty-six lashes. . . . The Census Returns for 1861 showed that one-third of the population of Scotland lived in single-roomed houses, and seven thousand nine hundred and sixty-four of these houses had no window. . . . In Port Glasgow a stable had been converted into a dwelling-house, and during the whole summer that stable contained eighty-three persons besides a horse. . . . In Glasgow fifty per cent of children died under five years of age. . . . In the first forty years of the nineteenth century some three hundred and fifty thousand strangers were suddenly huddled on the banks of the Clyde, where they suffered periodical decimation by typhus. . . . The Rev. Dr Lee testified that he had never seen such misery as in his parish, where the people were often without furniture, without everything, two married couples often sharing one room. In a single day he had visited seven houses in which there was not a bed, in some of them not even a heap of straw. Old people of eighty years slept on the board floor, nearly all slept in their day clothes. . . . In the Spring Circuit Court in Glasgow, 1864, Hugh Gray, for stealing a woollen lorry cover, gets eight years penal servitude; Mary Love, for stealing three yards of drugget from a hedge, gets six years; a man, Dogherty by name, gets three years for stealing a cloth cap from a shop door; Jane Campbell steals fourpence-ha'penny in copper, and gets fifteen months; but Alexander Still, for killing a man with a poker, gets off with six months. . . . Property was sacred, not life. . . . Cobbett says that the agricultural labourer is wholly at the mercy of his master; the man is a negro slave, worse off than the negro by many degrees. . . . Sheer hunger abode with the Scots miner in 1877. Wages were two shillings and sixpence to three shillings a day for two and three days a week, and the Fife and Clackmannan miners were locked-out altogether for six months rather than submit to a ten per cent reduction. . . . In 1840 children of eleven years worked from 5 a.m. to 5 p.m. A girl, Ellison Jack, of Loanhead Colliery, began at the age of eight to work from 2 a.m. till 1 p.m. or 2 p.m. " I go to bed at six to be ready for work next morning. I have had the strap when I didna do my bidding. I am very glad when my task is wrought as it sair fatigues." . . . The pit bottoms are like common sewers, slush and water, with an inclination of one in three, and along these common sewers the women, half-naked, crawl on hands and knees, harnessed like horses to their bogies of coals; little boys, aged four or five, sit all day in the darkness at the trap-doors, cold and shivering, begging for a candle-end for light. . . .'

These quotations are taken from Mr Thomas Johnston's *History of the Working Classes in Scotland*, a very valuable and extremely unpleasant book. It is, indeed, not so much a book as a literary machine-gun.

Every sentence is a bullet aimed at capitalism through the ages; and being thoroughly authenticated, the bullets find their mark. It is a work that not merely convinces one of the reality of the Class War in the Nineteenth Century, but enlists its readers on the side of the workers with irresistible compulsion.

The person of average intelligence, reading history for his own information and entertainment, is inevitably puzzled when he tries to envisage, in hues of their own perception, the life of the labouring classes during otherwise well-documented periods. Contemporary standards and current sensibility will incline him to the suspicion that life, for the great majority of people, has rarely been much more than an endurance test. So gloomy an interpretation, however, would be quite unwarranted, for there is a kind of intrinsic philosophy in man that fits him to encounter all but the most intemperate of climates and the most hostile environments. It is, perhaps, a sort of psychological gear-box that enables the trawl-fisherman, the factory-hand, and the millionaire of to-day to meet and survive, with organs of approximately the same specification, circumstances so widely different. And in the course of a couple of thousand years mankind's psychological gear-box has certainly included many other speeds than those now fitted: speeds, for instance, that enabled it to deal with semi-famines and the Inquisition, with service in the galleys and the burning of witches; speeds, beyond question, that gave him many sensations of happiness on ground that would appear impossible to us.

But there were certain periods in history when the psychological gear-box was too severely taxed, when life really did become intolerable, and before all other noise the sounds of wrath and weeping were significant. In the Nineteenth Century a new age of slavery came to Britain, and beneath the high-piled pomp and pride of industrial wealth there lived in squalid misery a more numerous multitude than ever before, verminous in the filthy tenements of industry, tortured and mis-shapen by fantastic toil, and starved by a ravenous and hypocritical tyranny. To Scotland the Industrial Revolution came with singular violence, and its attendant atrocities were aggravated not only by its geographical concentration, but by that head-strong rage which ever and again appears in Scotland, and by an hereditary sadism that was the product of our two misconceptions: patriotism-as-hatred, and religion-as-hatred. The poor people of Scotland suffered at the hands of their fellow Scots: that cannot be denied. But both rich and poor were governed by parliaments in Westminster—parliaments predominantly English—and as those parliaments were responsible for the welfare and behaviour of the whole people, so were they culpable for the misery of the serfs and the crimes of their masters. The obligations of authority are more numerous than its privileges.

It may be said that the English parliaments, being so far from Scotland, were ignorant of conditions there. That is not unlikely. And the moral is that authority, to be effective, must have its seat in the country it controls.

But squalor and wretchedness in the towns is only one side of a bad penny. On the other side is the savage picture of the Highland Clearances. The story of this fantastic experiment in hellishness has never been properly told, and we have little chance of ever reading an adequate history of it. For something like the strong grace of Theocritus would be needed to show the noble freedom and simplicity of the pastoral life the clansmen had led, and all the indignation of Swift could hardly describe the tortured penury they fell to, raking for shell-fish on a forbidden shore, or packed like felons in plague-ridden ships and sent without hope or provender to a cold and foreign land. Goya's pencil could draw the grotesque perversions of their oppressors, and Daumier depict the grinning hypocrisy of the parish ministers who defended the evictions as an act of God. Pope might rip to pieces the seamy pretensions to benevolence with which brutality was obligingly veneered; and someone like Marston, with an appetite for filth and Elizabethan vituperation, could deal with the factors who so diligently served their absent lords. But a coalition of Swift and Marston and Theocritus, of Goya and Pope and Daumier, is hardly likely, so figures must serve for the story: figures against a background of burning cottages, the sorrow of a noble people, and the damnable prosperity of oppression.

In the first half-dozen years of the Nineteenth Century some ten thousand people were driven out of the Western Highlands and Islands.[1] Between 1811 and 1820 fifteen thousand were evicted from Sutherlandshire.[2] Between 1831 and 1881 half the rural population of Argyllshire—thirty-nine thousand eight hundred and ninety-two victims—were turned out of their homes.[3] In the same period MacLeod

---

[1] Sheriff Brown's *Strictures and Remarks*, qu. by Johnson.
[2] Hugh Miller. [3] McKenzie's *Highland Clearances*.

evicted two thousand of his people from Skye, the Duke of Sutherland continued to depopulate his many acres, eighteen thousand crofters and their dependants were cleared out of Inverness-shire, the population of Ross-shire diminished by more than three thousand, Lochiel and Clanranald banished hundreds of their clansmen, and the long island of Lewis was lightened of two thousand four hundred and sixty souls.[1] Elsewhere, on the Borders as well as in the Highlands, uncountable families were driven from their native soil by evictions more piecemeal but as cruelly persistent.

And the reason for this wholesale misanthropy? A sudden affection for sheep. Humanity had depreciated, but wethers were rising in price. The old system of agriculture, under which the primary function of the soil was to support those who worked it, no longer seemed desirable when the landlords made the triple discovery that life in London, or even in Edinburgh, offered social amenities superior to any they had encountered on their estates; that these new-found pleasures were expensive; and that their cost might be met by breeding sheep instead of peasants. For England's wars with France and the

[1] McKenzie.

growth of Britain's industrial population had conveniently raised prices, and a protectionist policy that excluded all foreign cattle and sheep maintained them at an agreeable level. True, there came an appalling slump when Napoleon was at last disposed of, but in slumping times a tup can be made to do the work of two if fresh pastures are procured for the lambs he gets; and fresh pasture was easily found by evicting the people who tilled it. There was a certain amount of rioting, notably in Ross-shire and the Islands, when some of the crofters had the audacity to defend their property. There were unpleasant tales of starvation, of old men and children with no roof but the rain, and pregnant women with no bed but a ditch. There were stories of stinking emigrant ships that carried, willy-nilly and without provision for the future, unhappy people who had no English to a distant land that spoke no Gaelic. There was evidence that a people who had been proud and gracious and kindly and strong were now broken alike in spirit and in body. But despite these unpleasant circumstances the Highland landlords did very well out of their evictions till it became apparent that the earth will not for ever give its fruits without husbandry, and that other countries than Scotland were able to breed sheep. The grazing-grounds, to which centuries of labour had given sweetness and riches, turned sour under their countless wethers, and weeds and bracken overgrew the grass. And competitive mutton was brought in from oversea.

But the landlords were not without resources. When sheep grew unprofitable, sheep-runs dexterously became deer-forests, and deer, because of the pleasure people derived from shooting them, continued to pay the rent. Between 1883 and 1908 deer-forests in the five crofting counties increased their size by one and a quarter million acres, and Highland rent was paid by English brewers, Indian princes, American millionaires, Argentine ranchers, and international pickle-manufacturers. A sufficient number of the native population was retained to minister to cosmopolitan pleasure, to assist the strangers down steep places, to carry their guns and rifles, and to put their rods together.

Enlightened observers, especially in Scotland, began to detect a certain menial quality, a taint of the lackey, in our remnant Highlanders; and to comment unfavourably upon them. It was whispered they had lost their independence. It was said they were lazy, and would rather live on charity than work for their bread. Self-righteous and prosperous Lowlanders shook their bald heads over the Highlands. But in all conscience is it not a sign of indefeasible strength that one decent man or woman should still be able to live in a country that has been so treated? Is it not a proof of grace invincible that in remote corners of the Highlands you will still find bravery and exquisite manners and a great love of music? I say nothing of quotidian virtues—they are more common in the Highlands than in most places—but that people so long tortured and abominably oppressed should still retain some of the graces of life is proof that in the time of their happiness their life was endowed with virtue and beauty and dignity. And despite the deer and the grouse and the enforced servility, that life is not yet wholly extinct. A little flame remains, and could be blown upon. The deer-forests that once were sheep-runs, and before that were tilled with rude and primitive implements, could be reclaimed and again support such men as Chatham found ' upon the mountains of Caledonia, a race of heroes.'

But why should such a race breed again, you may ask, unless it is to be of economic value to the state? Because the true wealth of a country is to be counted in the happiness of its people, not in the millions in its

Treasury; because a hundred contented men are worth more than one wealthy man; because the Highlands of Scotland are too good to be left as a playground for rich visitors.

And what, you may ask again, has the tale of the Clearances and the deer-forests to do with English influence on Scottish affairs? They were English wars and an English economic policy that first made sheep more valuable than men; it was the pleasure to be found in English society—a cogent temptation—that made wealth seem so desirable to the Highland aristocracy; it was by a government predominantly English that Highland lairds and their factors were allowed to commit such atrocities over a long period of years, and though that government might be ignorant of the conditions, ignorance cannot excuse authority for failing to use the power it has assumed.

A circumstance of some interest in connexion with the history of the Clearances is that within recent years the Highlands have been re-invaded by human beings. It is, it is true, only a seasonal invasion, but it is vigorous, youthful, multi-hued, noisy, cheerful, vulgar, and every year more numerous. The invaders are called hikers, and complaints have been heard that they disturb the grouse and annoy the deer for whose

THE DARK AGES

sake the hills were made so large and the glens so lovely. But many of the hikers must be descendants of evicted Highlanders who sought refuge in the Lowland cities, and in contrast to those who complain of their behaviour, I find it very pleasant to think of them worrying the deer that replaced the sheep that dispossessed their fathers. I should like to see hikers, more numerous and brightly shirted than ever, on every mountain in Scotland; for if they scatter the grouse and pursue the deer far enough, the Highlands may again be available for the rightful heritors of earth: who are men.

V

ADDENDA AND CORRIGENDA

V
ADDENDA AND CORRIGENDA

THERE was a man called Paterson, a native of Dumfries, who conceived and gave form to the Bank of England, and being disappointed of a proper reward for this well-doing—or perhaps a victim to the promoter's itch—returned to Scotland and presently floated a company to occupy and exploit the Isthmus of Panama. With the aid of rhetoric, maps, and an almost religious fervour, he converted his romantic countrymen, and raised, in Scotland alone, the stupendous sum of £400,000.

It was, on the surface, a magnificent scheme. The Isthmus, it is true, was remote and few people knew anything about it. But for generations Scotsmen had been taught that only in heaven was their wealth, and Darien was nearer home than that. Darien, as the maps revealed, was the cross-roads of the world. The Pacific brought its cargoes to one shore, the Atlantic paid tribute to the other. Northwards were the new American colonies, and to the south lay the fabulous riches of the lower continent. Darien, indeed, was a promoter's paradise, and to a romantic people, emulous of their neighbour's growing empire, an irresistible bait. (Macaulay, who had neither sympathy for Paterson nor love for the Scots, could not bring himself to damn the project till he had empurpled page after page of his History with its splendid allurements.) But not only Scotland was captured: the City of London over-subscribed an English allotment, and Holland was also interested. Paterson looked for a moment—if time may be concertina'd—like a mixture of Raleigh and Rhodes, with, it may be, a regrettable tincture of Horatio Bottomley.

But there was a worm in the bud and frost in the air. Vested interests were hostile to the new company, and foreign policy looked freezingly upon it. The East India Company saw its monopoly threatened, and England feared the opposition of Spain. King William's government secured the withdrawal of English capital and forbade the participation of Holland. Scotland was left to pursue its vision alone, and neither its resources nor its experience were sufficient for so difficult a flight. The Darien scheme collapsed in dismal failure oversea and bankruptcy at home.

For this unhappiness England has often been blamed; but unfairly, I think. From the beginning the project was destined to calamitous failure, not so much at the probably hostile hands of Spain, as beneath the intemperate climate of Panama and the malignancy of the indigenous mosquito. England's abstention confined the catastrophe to Scotland; and the Scots, illogically, were embittered because their unhappiness was exclusive.

Another unfortunate incident during the reign of William the Dutchman was the massacre of the Macdonalds in Glencoe. William cannot be absolved from guilt in this matter, but far bloodier villains were the Earl of Breadalbane who contrived it, Dalrymple who commanded it, and the scoundrel Campbell of Glenlyon who executed it. In Glencoe, indeed, as in so many other places and at so many other times, Scotland's worst enemies were Scots. Yet the throne was English in whose shadow Glencoe became a synonym for treachery, and Darien a name for ruin; and fifteen years after the murder in the glen, nine years after the sailing of the doomed ships to Panama, when the Parliaments of the two countries were united, the people of Scotland were not unnaturally opposed to the unequal conjugation.

I do not think a description of the circumstances of the Union is necessary here. By the people it was detested; to the noblemen who had been bribed to bring it about—sometimes for a pound or two—it was doubtless as welcome as the sale of a score of cast ewes. A good account of the transaction may be found in Scott's *Tales of a Grandfather*, which should, perhaps, always be read in conjunction with any modern statement of Scottish history: for no one who writes to-day is so capable either of relishing or conveying its romantic aspects, and for all we know the romantic view may be as important, and as true, as our disgusted vision of coincident misery. It does not seem probable, in our present disillusionment, but we may be wrong: I should like to think that we are.

Scott, however, has no illusions about the Union except one: despite the unwillingness of the Scots to be united with England, he believed that union was for their ultimate good. And in some ways, of course, he was right.

Let us count our blessings. It will be a pleasant change from contemplating past miseries, and possibly a wise corrective. For misery has a greater survival value than happiness, and history, that preserves in a limbeck or a reliquary the blood of battles and the iniquity of the great, forgets how many golden lads and girls spent Flodden's night in blissful, leg-locked sleep; how many plump merchants made an unexpected guinea the day Charles Edward turned home from Derby; how many honest housewives thought more of a well-basted fowl, and a good husband's gratitude for it, than of John Knox's sermons; how much ale was drunk in despite of the iron law of wages; and that cheerfulness and kindliness were not all killed by Kirk Sessions. Half a millennium hence historians may write of 1935 as a village on the slope of a smoking volcano. They may say that all Europe was an armed camp, and the threat of war occluded all other thoughts. They may speak of the millions of men who were unemployed and had no hope of employment. They may describe our desperate race to re-arm, and our futile conferences to keep the peace. They may quote statistics to show that children were undernourished, and most of their parents cancerous. They may see the Class Struggle as we see the Wars of the Roses, and with horror discuss our miseducation, our music, and our mass hysterias. But what will they know, these grave historians, of our sweet pillow-whispering and our dinner-tables, our love for Garbo, our joy in sailing-boats, our excursions in charabancs, our winning shillings on the Glasgow Rangers? Nothing at all.

Count, then, our blessings. . . .

It was but the other morning that I lay too long in a hot bath and thought of Mr Neville Chamberlain. His several budgets, by most politic plumbing, had stopped the leakage in our financial system, and my chance of quotidian bathing under lavish taps—could I but write another novel or two—seemed secure for several years. A hideous multitude of houses, it is true, were still uncomforted by the luxuries of plumbing that I enjoyed, but the very worst of the slums, in Glasgow and Motherwell and Dundee, were neither so dark nor so rancid nor so lousily populous as they had been eighty years before. The world was a little cleaner than it used to be. Life, in Britain at any rate, was a little more merciful than it had been. We did not leave our unemployed—our brace of million unemployed—to starve to death; we kept them half-alive, and half a livelihood was better than no bread at all. Nor were children with the milk still in their bones driven to work, to be stunted and twisted and ruined, in factories and mines as they had been in the days of our god-fearing grandfathers; their minds, instead of their bodies, might be somewhat distorted in our national schools; but that would not worry them much. And tinned pineapple and fish and chips were available for stomachs that had turned in utter weariness from centuries of oatmeal and salted herrings. The world, I said—lying in my hot bath—was more comfortable than it used to be, and therefore better; and since an English government has been blamed for permitting the squalid tyranny of the Industrial Revolution and the merciless evictions in the Highlands, so must other English governments be praised for effecting these large improvements in our lot. . . .

For a moment or two—the window was open and a cold little breeze blew in and pushed aside the warm steam—for a moment my optimism faltered, and I remembered an Irish doctor, a gynecologist, who had enthusiastically praised Glasgow from a professional point of view. He was full of admiration for the opportunities it offered to a student of midwifery. 'It's a fine place,' he said. 'Yes, indeed it is. Just walk about the streets and you'll see deformities and narrow pelvises all round you. Little undersized comical beggars and oddities, you know. Oh, it's a grand place to be. You get first-rate experience there. . . .'

But eighty years ago there were more dreadful deformities on every street than we can ever see now. Eighty years ago there were sabre shins and tubercular hips where now there is mild rickets only. The great pox laid noses in ruins and the small pox hideously pitted round young cheeks where now ill nourishment may rot a few teeth and pale the complexion. Typhus killed where influenza now discomforts. Children in countless thousands died at the breast, while now they live to go on the dole. . . . I turned on the hot tap, and said firmly, 'The world is more comfortable than it used to be.' I passed my tongue reflectively round my teeth, and felt the smooth fillings that had preserved them, and some excellent bridge-work that counterfeited their lost efficiency; and I thought, 'Had I lived some eighty years ago, progressive decay would have brought me infinite pain, and my pleasure in eating would have been ruined by clumsy ill-fitting dentures. But thanks to an admirable dentist, caries has been circumvented, and I have retained my appetite.' My dentist, moreover, was trained in England. Let credit be given where credit is due.

Were I a miner, thin-ribbed from meagre wages

ADDENDA AND CORRIGENDA

and the quota system, I should be less philosophical. But had I been a Scottish miner a hundred years ago, or a little more, I should have been, quite literally, a slave. From the impotence of serfdom to the hardships of freedom on thirty-two shillings a week is a step in the right direction, though scarcely a long enough step. But the credit for it is England's, and the credit for a hundred comparable steps: because for the last two hundred years England has governed us.

Let us count our blessings; for historians will forget them.

The greatest is life, despite its inconveniences; and during the last century twenty years, perhaps, has been added to the life of a working man, and the slum-born infants whose advent coincided with the Silver Jubilee of King George V will spend comfortable days in comparison with the wet verminous bundles who were expected to become subjects of Victoria and Albert the Good. We have a social conscience now. We are emerging from the Dark Ages. Our eyes are opening, like Cophetua's, to the shape of humanity beneath the grey rags of poverty, and the barbarism of the Nineteenth Century appears almost as remote from us as witch-burning or crusading hatred of Mahound.

ADDENDA AND CORRIGENDA

They are English governments that have put humanitarianism into practice. Their predecessors permitted the atrocities of the last centuries, but contemporary authority has done much—though often unwillingly—to mitigate that destitution which is the inevitable by-blow of large industrialism; and much to provide the victims of industrialism with compensatory recreation.

For the anæsthesia of doles, pensions, and cheap amusement; for longer life and cleaner towns; for sensibility and a quicker conscience, let us thank our English legislators and teachers.

VI

THE QUESTION OF CULTURE

VI
THE QUESTION OF CULTURE

'YET what the Romans did to other nations, was in a great degree done by Cromwell to the Scots; he civilized them by conquest, and introduced by useful violence the arts of peace. I was told at Aberdeen that the people learned from Cromwell's soldiers to make shoes and to plant kail.'

So says Dr Johnson in his *Journey to the Western Islands*; and having glanced unhappily at the vacuum that must have preceded cabbage, he queries the benefaction of the cobbler, and discovers in the culture of Scotland a quality unique in his experience. 'I know not,' he writes, 'whether it be not peculiar to the Scots to have attained the liberal, without the manual arts, to have excelled in ornamental knowledge, and to have wanted not only the elegancies, but the conveniencies of common life. Literature soon after its revival found its way to Scotland, and from the middle of the sixteenth century, almost to the middle of the seventeenth, the politer studies were very diligently pursued. . . . Yet men thus ingenious and inquisitive were content to live in total ignorance of the trades by which human wants are supplied, or to supply them by the grossest means. Till the Union made them acquainted with English manners, the culture of their lands was unskilful, and their domestick life unformed; their tables were coarse as the feasts of Esquimeaux, and their houses filthy as the cottages of Hottentots.

'Since they have known that their condition was capable of improvement their progress in useful knowledge has been rapid and uniform. What remains to be done they will quickly do, and then wonder, like me, why that which was so necessary and so easy was so long delayed. But they must be for ever content to owe to the English that elegance and culture, which, if they had been vigilant and active, perhaps the English might have owed to them.'

These paragraphs are like a stone wall with a little window in the middle of it. Complacently ignorant of history's economic aspect, Johnson fails to see that Scotland's lack of the elegancies and decencies of common life was due to the sterilization, the paralysis,

THE QUESTION OF CULTURE

the mutilation of English and internecine warfare. Whenever Scotland discovered a decade of peace, the conveniencies of life began to multiply; but no sooner had Scotland achieved a little prosperity, a little comfort even, than dissension broke it asunder or an English army came to trample on it. Cromwell's garrisons reduced Scotland to bankruptcy: the Cromwellian psalm-singing Ogpu cost £40,000 a month, of which only a tenth could be raised locally, for the very good reason that a year's maintenance of the garrisons was almost equal to the whole monetary wealth of Scotland;[1] and that was an extravagant price to pay for some skill in shoe-making and market-gardening, and the introduction to Inverness of an accent that 'has been long considered as peculiarly elegant.'

But in spite of Johnson's marmoreal impercipience, the little window in the middle of it throws a strong and interesting light. That Scotland had once attained the liberal arts in preference and priority to the manual arts—or even that Scotland had acquired the reputation of excelling in ornamental knowledge at the expense of quotidian conveniencies—are matters for curious

[1] Fifty years later all coin circulating in Scotland was called in; the sum collected was £411,117. Chambers estimated that £150,000 remained in circulation.

speculation. The contemporary ethos of Scotland is practical, mundane, *faubourien*. Mr George Blake, in an excellent account of Scotland to-day, has very shrewdly remarked that the Lowland working classes 'have the sense of all but æsthetic values.' And the sensibility of their social superiors is not seldom confined to the trajectory of a golf ball, their intellectual interest to the permutation and combination of trumps in a hand at contract bridge. Where, then, has gone that passionate care for the elegant superfluities of existence, for the decorations and the spiritual arts of life? What staring summer's heat has consumed those *neiges d'antan*?

For three hundred years the social and economic life of Scotland had been conditioned by the Kirk, the Industrial Revolution, and England. Has the life that we see through Johnson's little window been stifled by the one, destroyed by the other, or diverted by the third? Or did it never exist? Perhaps one should answer the last question first.

It may be said, with no more than a suspicion of rhetoric to invalidate the statement, that Scotland is the home of lost cultures. Perhaps the oldest surviving verse in the common tongue is Wyntoun's lament:

THE QUESTION OF CULTURE

' Quhen Alysandyr oure kyng was dede,
   That Scotland led in luve and le,
Away wes sons off ale and brede,
   Off wyne and wax, of gamyn and gle:
Oure gold wes changyd into lede . . .'

Gone, too, were scholarship and schoolmen, and architecture ceased. Scotland had felt and responded to the contemporary vitality of Europe, and was propagating a corresponding life of its own; and in the War of Independence it said good-bye to this, the first of its nascent cultures.

But after about seventy years of fighting, something like peace returned for a while to Scotland, and literature, naturally enough, began to show its face again, and new churches and castles rose from the scattered stones. The names of a hundred lost tales and poems survive from this period—literature's infant mortality rate, in all countries, almost persuades one to compare history with a slum—and the good historian Barbour, sound in heart and head, appears. In the first James Scotland had a king whom Chaucer had taught to be a poet, and the fourth James, himself a scholar and a musician, had for subjects the great makars, Dunbar and Henryson and Gavin Douglas. With them to use it, the Scottish tongue acquired an amazing strength. The makars have commonly been called Chaucerians, but in some ways they were rather pre-Elizabethans. Like Marlowe's, their vocabulary had the seemingly inexhaustible and ever-growing riches of a new-found Golconda. They had the many-sidedness of men whose minds were alive in all quarters. They had such a frank delight in their art that, though an art of such high accomplishment, it was still a plaything. It was the art of the Renaissance, and under James IV the Renaissance made a brave start in Scotland. But Flodden checked it, and the Reformation killed it.

Dr Johnson refers to Scotland's pursuit of the politer studies 'from the middle of the sixteenth century, almost to the middle of the seventeenth.' There were, within this period, translations into Scots verse of Livy and Petrarch and Ariosto; and Napier of Merchiston invented a calculating machine and discovered the use of logarithms. But Johnson was probably thinking of the Latinists, Wilson of Aberdeen, Buchanan, and Arthur Johnstone, who was Charles I's physician: Buchanan is said to have been the finest Latin poet since Latin was written in Rome: he was certainly a most accomplished liar in the common tongue. Johnson would also have had in mind Drummond of Hawthornden,

THE QUESTION OF CULTURE

a lonely and unrepresentative poet; and the magnificent Urquhart.

But Urquhart and Drummond wrote in English. So, to a great extent, did Knox. Scotland was reading by then an English translation of the Bible; and the Confession of Faith, the Catechism, and the Metrical Psalms that came in the middle of the seventeenth century were English. Another culture had been lost.

The Scottish tongue no longer spoke a national language. It spoke a dialect, and that which had been its proper pronunciation of Scots became in English merely a Scottish accent. It is true that the remnant dialect, with a stiffening of archaic forms, was later to be fashioned into the most popular of all Scottish contributions to literature: but the language of Burns was an artefact, a literary convention. I am not decrying his genius—it would not matter if I did—but his language, in comparison with Dunbar's, is patently a slight and precarious thing. He will slide easily into English; he depends on a literal representation of a northern accent, the mere substitution of commas for consonants; he constantly betrays, as Dunbar never does, a paucity of rhyming material that comes from the paucity of his whole language.

Because, of course, it was no longer a language. It was only a dialect, and, incidentally, the means of showing what marvellous things can be made with a broken tool in the hands of genius.

Now this destruction of Scotland's language—the language of Henryson and Dunbar—was, from the literary and in a larger sense the spiritual point of view, a tragedy. It was a language of great richness and amazing flexibility. It was built on so broad and various a foundation that obviously it was capable of enormous growth. It could produce all the necessary sounds: contempt and joy, laughter and hatred and easy dialogue; it could interpret the essential phases of the spirit: reflexion and exaltation, judgment and clear vision and delight. It was quite different from English, and it would have kept the soul and manners of Scotland different from those of England: for in the beginning of everything is the word. But it was defeated, and ruined, and it vanished. And though in exchange for it Scotsmen were to receive a language that holds within its wide geography everything from the crystal spring to thunder in the mountains, from the back street to the clear debate of counsellors, yet for Scotland it was a tragedy that its own tongue, that would have compassed as much and might have found a few unstruck notes as well, should have been so irretrievably lost.

During the last few years in Scotland there have been signs, albeit small and confused, of a certain awareness of this tragedy. There has been some propaganda on behalf of what is occasionally called the Doric, or Braid Scots, and some people say it should be taught in the schools. No good argument, however, can be adduced for this project. The Braid Scots of to-day is, at its best, a local dialect; at its weakest, merely a local accent. It is, moreover, rapidly decaying, as the usage and the voice of the towns infect the adjacent country. No dialect, apparently, can survive an urban life. A rural accent and a rural dialect are generally pleasing to the ear and not unsatisfying to the mind, but transplant them to a town and they soon become meagre and hard and mean.—Compare the generous voice of Perthshire or the Borders with the whining of Dundee and of Edinburgh.—Now speech is something so delicately and almost transparently alive that it cannot be artificially preserved, and it cannot be patched. It can, however, be changed. And so long as Scottish life is predominantly an urban life, the only sensible change is towards the mean to which three hundred years of history have pointed: that is, towards standard English. Let the initial tragedy be forgotten, and let us be thankful that we have, as a substitute for our lost tongue, a tongue so graceful and well-endowed. There are Scots, I know, who will say that English is a handicap to the free expression of their thoughts, and that while they might run like Achilles in the Doric, they must limp like a cripple in the Southron talk. But as all Scotland of to-day, and our fathers and grandfathers, cut their teeth on English printed words, I take leave to doubt such statements. It is generally a bad workman who complains of his tools, and poor golfers who say they would do better with other clubs.

If, however, the balance of life were to swing back from the town to the country, then the dialects might well be worth the saving. For country talk is comely, and whatever is comely deserves life. But in that case there would be no need for scholastic formalin or artificial respiration. Environment would nurture and preserve the intonation, and as many words as were requisite for rural needs—which, if we exclude intellectual interests, are larger and more searching than those of the town—would supply themselves, and become moulded to a natural voice. A rural dialect is nourished by its own fields and is a language in a nutshell. An urban dialect is merely the detritus of a language, and is worth nothing. Its idiom is debased, its habitat the kitchen and the pavement. It will translate *Experientia docet* into ' Sook it and see.'

A more interesting and a much more intelligent attitude to the drowned Atlantis of Scots is that of Mr C. M. Grieve.[1] Mr Grieve, very sensibly, is more interested in the classical tongue than its surviving dialects. Rightly or wrongly he believes that current English is somewhat pale, flaccid, and nerveless; and whoever will examine contemporary American may well agree that colloquial English, for any incisive purpose, is a blunted blade compared with that. Returning for strength, therefore, to his native rock, Mr Grieve has quarried some fine granitic words out of the makars; and his earlier poetry had a power that completely over-rode its necessary slight obscurity. But Mr Grieve's recent tendency—or so it seems— has been towards an English rather than a Scottish norm. His earlier poetry was a literary and highly artificial Scots; and it was the best poetry Scotland had produced since Burns. But as his later work has grown philosophical rather than lyrical, he has been

[1] Or Hugh McDiarmid.

compelled to use English, the fully developed language, with a stiffening, not only of Scots words, but of German. His literary Scots, despite its power and ingenuity, was insufficient for any purpose larger than the expression of fairly simple emotions. No man, out of dictionaries and his own virtue, can make a whole language. A language requires communal effort. And when Mr Grieve was impelled to present ideas instead of images, to argue rather than to sing, to describe not a tree but a concept, he had to write in English. But, like Dunbar, he pirated ripe words from other tongues, and stuck them in wherever they might do good. And that, I think, is a very sensible and laudable device. For in any language there is a kind of metabolism, and so a hunger for food. Certain words and expressions are worn out, and disappear; and to keep the body plump and strong it needs new nourishment. At the time of its greatest achievements English was pirating right and left, and inventing in the middle. But for the last thirty or forty years English appears to have been on a diet. It has either been slimming or rationalizing. A few engineering technicalities have been added to our colloquial vocabulary, with a handful of psychological and medical terms, and some convenient euphemisms for diplomatic occasions; but it is very doubtful whether these accretions have been sufficient to make good the inevitable loss by attrition or time's digestive juice. It is certain that neither current slang nor the reported speeches of our politicians have the variety of diction, the dignity or vividness of some of their predecessors. We have, perhaps, been living too much on our capital. English has grown more insular as Britain has become more imperialist. The political extension of England has been accompanied by a verbal shrinkage. We are prone to despise other tongues because those who use them are politically or socially inferior to us. Our colonial traffic with savage and primitive peoples has occupied us at the expense of communion with civilized nations. And so English, instead of growing ever fatter and stronger, has become a little faded and wizened. The current intellectual preference for a plain, level, unexciting form of writing is due to a subconscious recognition of this: it indicates, on the part of writers, a very decent determination to write within their income: we can't be extravagant, so we praise and cultivate economy.

But Mr Grieve advocates a policy of literary inflation, and as similar policies have been so advantageous in the past, a new issue of Scottish words might well be

THE QUESTION OF CULTURE

useful at present. Much of Dunbar's language consists of hard vivid names for things: it can be admirably descriptive of visual and auditory impressions: and new words of this kind—immediate, first-hand, sensory—are, perhaps, what we need most. But the existing constitution of English must be maintained, because we have no other to put in its place, nor is it likely that anyone could invent a better.

Before discussing a third culture that rose in Scotland, and died too soon, it may be interesting to consider one of those English importations for which the Kirk was responsible. I mean the Metrical Version of the Psalms, which was brought in triumph home from the Assembly of Divines at Westminster. These melancholy, illiterate, and limping verses have been sung for generations in nearly every church in Scotland. Children of tender years, their minds responsive as clay to the potter's thumb, have been forced to sing:

> 'Lord, Thou shalt early hear my voice:
>   I early will direct
> My pray'r to Thee; and, looking up,
>   An answer will expect.' [1]

In praise of a Creator who, having created so largely and so handsomely, could hardly be ignorant of craftsmanship or indifferent to art, they sang:

---
[1] Ps. v. 3.

THE QUESTION OF CULTURE

>'That there is not a God, the fool
>   doth in his heart conclude:
>They are corrupt, their words are vile;
>   Not one of them doth good.'[1]

To the Lord Whose ears delighted in the morning stars singing together, the pious people of Scotland sang:

>'All ends of th' earth remember shall
>   and turn the Lord unto;
>All kindreds of the nations
>   to Him shall homage do:
>Because the kingdom to the Lord
>   doth appertain as His;
>Likewise among the nations
>   the Governor He is.'[2]

The metre, competently handled, does very well indeed for the adventures of John Gilpin. But the Westminster Divines, having elected to make it the vehicle of mankind's most lofty aspirations and sublime conception, handled it with the awful ineptitude of a back-street ballad-monger; and the Kirk of Scotland approved and adopted their work. The effect of these irreverent jingles on the literary taste of Scotland is incalculable. Ears acclimatized, by the inevitable repetition of Sabbath worship, to the hobble and trot of the verses, and the holy moaning of the tunes that

[1] Ps. xiv. 1. [2] Ps. xxii. 27, 28.

reined them in, must have been sadly thickened against more subtle cadences; and the unambitious monotony of Scottish poetasters may well be one of the more obvious results of so many anæsthetic Sundays. Scotland forgot and survived the injuries of Flodden and Pinkie and Solway Moss, but our spirit has hardly recovered from the reiterated indignity of having to sing:

> 'What profit is there in my blood,
> When I go down to pit?
> Shall unto Thee the dust give praise?
> Thy truth declare shall it?'

That verses such as these—and there are hundreds just as bad—should have been imported from England when the ink of *Lycidas* was scarcely dry, when Herbert was lately dead, while Vaughan and Marvell were writing, is one of those ironies, delightful or appalling according to the mood one is in, that give history the semblance of literature, and incline one to the belief that God—*pace* Professor Jeans and his mathematical deity—is a dramatist of the Shakespearian kind, a dramatist contemptuous of the unities, superbly capable of combining the elements of farce and high comedy and searing tragedy into one—dare I borrow from the cinema's publicity men?—into one sizzling whole. Even to the supers life is frequently delicious;

THE QUESTION OF CULTURE

but to the spectators it must be magnificent, if, as piety surely insists, one may ascribe to the supernal audience a high degree of intelligence.

> 'Shall unto Thee the dust give praise?
> Thy truth declare shall it?'—

Is there not a resemblance between this English gift and the gifts of England to savage Africa and the idyllic islands of the South Seas: such gifts, out of England's treasury, as bowler hats and the common cold, and gin and cotton underwear? It is not unnatural that so great a civilization should have had so many regrettable by-products; it is a pity, however, that most of them have been exported.

But I have been diverted from the tale of Scotland's abortive cultures. We have seen how its mediæval culture, of which our knowledge admittedly is somewhat inferential, disappeared under the hammer-strokes, and their echoes, of the first Edward; we have noticed the renaissance, under James IV, that was stunned by English wars and stifled by the Reformation; and we must now observe the remarkable liveliness of the Eighteenth Century.

This was a manifold and multifarious liveliness. It was liveliness so diverse in expression as to merit the larger name of life. It included the Ramsays and

David Hume; Fergusson and Adam Smith; Smollett and Boswell and Thomson's *Seasons*; the begetter of *Ossian* and the author of *A Man of Feeling*. It comprised a new and successful conception of horticulture, and the superb portrait-painting of Raeburn. It gave Voltaire reason to complain that 'it is from Scotland we receive rules of taste in all the arts, from the epic poem to gardening.' It coincided with, if it did not embrace, a spirited and accomplished output of Gaelic poetry; it found room for the mechanical ingenuity of James Watt; it produced a virile and sometimes virulent criticism; it culminated in the lyric genius of Burns, in the scholarship and vast romantic creativeness of Scott.

Scotland again had its head above the water. Its eyes were searching, its ears open, and its tongue loquacious. And this period of freedom and creative activity was contemporary with the rule of the Moderates in the Kirk. The significance of this is obvious. No art could flourish under the tyranny of Calvinistic presbyteries, but as soon as the presbyteries felt the new air from France, of intellectual tolerance and philosophic doubt, and their discipline grew easier, then the arts, as though waiting only for spring, came multi-coloured out of hard ground. Once more the ornaments of life and its liberal avocations were cultivated with that enthusiasm which led Dr Johnson to believe that in Scotland there existed a peculiar preference for things of the mind, a singular contempt for material welfare. And once again a hard-won culture was to be ruined and laid waste.

Now observe, for a moment, a pretty coincidence. The French Revolution created a new and infective focus of enthusiasm. The people and the Kirk of Scotland were touched by the warm current, the Moderates presently gave way to the Evangelicals, and the pulpits gave voice to ardent gloom. Religion of a kind—Calvinism in a new coat—asserted again its old authority, and the ministers, by directing the eyes of the people to that heaven whose patent was their own property, prevented them from looking too closely at the earth beneath: where, by this time, abominable things were happening. With darkness and with vermin, like the plagues of Egypt, the Industrial Revolution came to Scotland. Speculation, that used to mean intellectual enquiry, became a synonym for financial activity. The towns grew like ulcers, and like ulcers they drained the life of the surrounding country. On the analogue of Joseph, who cornered Egypt's wheat, it became a sign of virtue to be rich. Leisure was frowned upon, and vanished. For six days did men labour, and on the seventh they pulled down the blinds of their windows —at the minister's command—lest looking out in idleness they should see the desolation they had made of life. Bemused by sermons, the rich forgot charity; ravenous for wealth, they were ignorant of beauty; and burdened by an intolerable conscience, they denied their own and everybody else's right to any but the most concealed and curtained of pleasures. From such an atmosphere the arts fled like flowers and happiness from the Western Front. One art remained, but a conservative rather than a liberal art, and that —perhaps it should be called a talent—was a talent for domestic enjoyment. Mr George Blake, who knows the Scottish ethos as well as anybody living, has said, 'Scottish life centres to a remarkable extent round the hearth and home. It is a race domesticated quite beyond the ordinary.'

The home, of course, like Church and Bible Class, was a refuge from the strenuous ugliness of industrial life. It might be ugly enough, but it was peaceful and private. And when literature returned to Scotland, it was a literature of escape that became popular.

THE QUESTION OF CULTURE

Now of these three cultures—Mediæval, Renaissance, and Eighteenth Century—the first owed almost everything to an English princess, to her sons and grandsons, and to their Anglo-Norman influence; the second, despite the name of *Chaucerians* that has been given to its literary protagonists, owed very little to England; and the third used English— sometimes with difficulty—for its written language, and progressively favoured the English spoken word. It was, in a way, a deliberated culture. It employed a language that was not wholly native to it. It turned its back decisively on the remnant dialects of Scotland. It made English obligatory in polite writing and in polite society. It changed the whole sound and appearance of things. But it had no roots, and when it died, beneath the locusts of industrialism and the Calvinist evangel, the disappearance of Scotland, save as a geographical expression, appeared to be imminent. Its life, as an independent expression of life, diminished rapidly. National consciousness so far degenerated that presently its only externalizations were music-hall jokes; a grim determination, on the part of individuals, to prosper in life and compensate their feeling of inferiority with wealth and power; a sentimental attitude to Loch Lomond; an illiterate reverence of

Burns; a pathetic affection for such words as *pawky* and *canny*—the kitchen refuse of a noble tongue—and the qualities they described. In 1902 the eldest son of Queen Victoria was crowned King of Great Britain and Ireland as Edward VII: the ordinal implied that all the previous Edwards, from the pestilent first of that name to the unfortunate sixth, had equally been kings of all Britain: but so unreal and shadowlike a thing had Scotland become that his title was accepted with only a murmur of dissent. Scotland had once been poor and proud. Now it was neither.

Sir Walter Scott had done something to encourage this English digestion of its old enemy. Such was his genius that he made Scotland popular in England, and England well thought of in Scotland. He was, very sensibly, an Anglophile. Warmly devoted to the better things in his own country, he also perceived, being wise and clear of vision, the manifold beauties of England, the abundant virtue and the charming qualities of the English people, and the richness of English life. And having sold the romance and the quiddities and the sterling worth of Scotland to English readers, he sold the loveliness and the delight of England to his Scottish public. Nobody has ever done more for our mutual benevolence than Sir Walter.

Then commerce and industry began their lopsided unification of the two countries; and the wealthy bourgeoisie of Scotland became aware, not merely of the wealth of England, but of its social advantages. The aura of the bourgeoisie is snobbery, and snobbery spoke with an English accent. The English schools did something to a boy that no Scots grammar school could do: something rather incomprehensible, but very gratifying in its effects: they touched him with apostolic hands, and he received that untroubled assurance of his importance which is the birthright of aristocracy. In time their virtue became somewhat attenuated, and in the newer establishments it was hardly authentic; but even a fictitious importance was not unwelcome to many. And Oxford and Cambridge were beyond question superior in all ways to the universities of Scotland. So Cambridge and Oxford and the public schools began to draw to themselves such part of the youth of Scotland as could afford to be received by them.

Now it is neither my purpose nor my desire to depreciate the English public schools; and for Oxford and for Cambridge I have nothing but reverence,

But in two ways their effect on Scotland has been unfortunate. In the first place they substituted an English culture for that diversity of cultures with which, in earlier times, Scotland had always been in contact. In earlier days Scottish students had gone for instruction to France and Holland, and farther afield. But now they all went to England. (In a like fashion their cousins and brothers enlisted or took commissions only in the English army, where aforetime they had done their soldiering with France and Sweden, with Germany and with Russia.) By reason of its association with England, Scotland became insular. Its political frontier was broken down, and its mind was walled up. Geographical or political enlargement, beyond certain limits, is nearly always accompanied by intellectual shrinkage.

In the second place, by taking from Scottish schools and universities many who might have stayed in Scotland—had English education been more inaccessible and less fashionable—England has deprived the Scottish academies of students who would have been valuable in a much-needed way. Those who go to England for their education are, obviously, the sons of well-to-do parents. They enjoy, therefore, a certain economic independence. Their behaviour, then, is likely to be less trammelled by that fear of imminent disaster, if they fail to satisfy their instructors, which broods over the great majority of students at the Scots universities. Being without economic fear, their minds are free—if their minds are of that sort—to explore the elegancies as well as the essentials of learning; to pursue the liberal arts with a liberal rather than a pragmatic spirit; to put forth, as well as statutory blooms, bright flowers of their own device. It is students of this kind that the Scots universities need most urgently; for though in many ways their teaching is admirable, the official curriculum takes up too much of the picture. The typical Scots student is like a man with a heavy hod on his back climbing a long ladder: the hod is economic fear, the rungs of the ladder are daily lectures, and the top—which often rests against a schoolhouse window—is his final examination. Now when practically all the students are laden with similar hods, and when all are convinced of the necessity of reaching the top in a given time, the university's view of life and learning is bound to be rigidly confined to the rungs ahead and in front of it. But if young men who have no hod to carry, or a light and convenient hod—some of those who go to Oxford and Cambridge—were to

THE QUESTION OF CULTURE

stay in Scotland, they would have time to regard the surrounding country, or jump down from the ladder and increase their agility on the broader earth about them; and then talk to their heavily burdened companions of what they had seen or learned. Their economic freedom, enabling them to take a larger and more independent view of scholarship and citizenship, would enliven and aerate the whole university. They would have the time and the opportunity to theorize beyond the narrow limits imposed on theories by examination; and their speculation would be like an oxygenating draught.

But even were these lightly burdened students to do no more than familiarize their fellows with the attitudes and conventions of a more fortunate social level, they would still be useful. For ninety per cent of Scots students live in a severely limited environment. Their parents are poor, their homes of necessity are without culture, and though their morals are excellent their manners are unpolished. And a good manner—to take no higher estimate—has commercial importance. How often has one heard it said of a Scots student, 'Yes, he seems to know his work all right, but he's too hairy about the heels. I'm afraid he wouldn't suit the job at all.'

THE QUESTION OF CULTURE

Such a mode of judgment may or may not be regrettable. But it exists, and there is cause for its existence, and the cause will remain so long as the Scottish universities attract only those who cannot afford to go elsewhere. If the remaining aristocracy of Scotland, and the still prosperous bourgeoisie, were to abjure the English universities and send their sons to Aberdeen and Glasgow, to St Andrews or to Edinburgh, they would benefit the youth of all Scotland. We cannot improve our rustic manners, nor slough our parochialism, when they who might instruct us by their superior example, and those whom more prosperous experience has liberalized and made urbane, desert us and betake themselves over the Border.

It is obvious that no country can nurture a national culture when its cultural instincts merely express themselves in flight. If Scotland is to survive more widely than in the minds of cartographers, then some anti-magnet to the English lodestone must speedily be found. It may, perhaps, be found in the political aspirations of Scottish Nationalists; or in the little current recrudescence of interest in the arts so hopefully called a Scottish Renaissance. These movements both spring from the realization that the national life of Scotland has been drained to a dangerously low level, and from a belief that Scotland, as a national entity, is worth preservation. The response of the Scottish people to them will show whether such a belief is justified.

VII
BIBULOUS INTERLUDE

VII

BIBULOUS INTERLUDE

THE Rubaiyat of Omar Khayyam, I believe, is not much in the fashion nowadays, and in a world whose average mental age is barely that of puberty—consider our universal admiration of Mickey Mouse; our minstrels who croon to us in the milky vocables of the crèche; and the foreign policy of great nations—that is hardly a matter for surprise. Omar is a little too old for us. He was probably about nineteen when he wrote his charming quatrains: his exuberant despair, his cynicism like a plume, his delight in the moment of actuality, are surely the bright feature of very early manhood? Be that as it may, there are times when, like him, I wonder what the vintners buy one half so precious as the stuff they sell. And at such times, in such a mood, I think with special bitterness of the present injustice to whisky.

The duty on whisky is now seventy-two shillings and sixpence per proof gallon. This means that every purchaser of a twelve-and-sixpenny bottle of whisky pays a tax of eight shillings and fivepence ha'penny to a government that is doing its best to ruin the industry whose products give him so much pleasure. For obviously it is a penal tax, and the result of it has been to reduce the number of Scottish distilleries from about a hundred and thirty in 1920 to fifteen in 1933. Let us consider, for no more than a moment, the economic aspects of this reduction. A distillery may use three thousand quarters of barley in a working year. In 1930 distillers used three and three-quarter million hundredweights of barley; in 1933 they used only half-a-million hundredweights. Now distilling is a Scottish industry, and to penalize it in this way means the penalizing of Scottish farmers and Scottish miners—a distillery will burn five hundred tons a year of the best coal—as well as the general mutilation of pleasure. In June 1926 Scottish farmers grew 122,000 acres of barley; in 1933 the acreage had fallen to less than 60,000.[1] Nor can the Exchequer defend the legislation that has produced this impoverishment of Scotland by showing that it has fostered the wealth of Britain as a whole. It has

---

[1] These and some of the preceding figures I obtained from a letter written and published by Mr Brodie Hepburn.

BIBULOUS INTERLUDE

impaired it. The tax on whisky is manifestly a stupid tax. It appears also to be a malevolent tax. One cannot believe it would continue at its monstrous figure if distilling were an English industry—or should one call it an art? For some little ago the tax on beer, which is predominantly an English product, was considerably reduced, with resulting benefit to the English brewers and hop-growers.

But let economics and politics be forgotten, and think of whisky rather as part of Scotland's contribution to humanity, as claret is a great part of the munificence of France. Now the varieties of claret are innumerable, from the thin but honest simplicity of a tenpenny Médoc to the rich yet subtle enchantment of the first growths of the three great Châteaux, in which perfume and flavour and bloom, divisible yet undivided, are as three aspects of perfection in Perfection. This multiplicity of delight, conveyed in the single word claret, is known or acknowledged by all. But to the majority of people whisky is merely whisky, an amber spirit unfairly diluted by obtuse authority, in a bottle whose shape is more often variable than its contents. How wrong is this judgment! And how shameful that there should be grounds for it! For it cannot be denied that under recent legislation, and as

BIBULOUS INTERLUDE

a result of commercial arrangements to survive it, there is to-day an undistinguished monotony in many brands. Yet if distillers were fairly treated, and encouraged to take a pleasure and a pride in their art, they could produce whisky as variable in flavour and character as claret.

Even to-day, under the staggering handicap of the existing duty, there is more variety in it than is ever suspected by the unhappy multitude that asks, without specification, for 'whisky and soda': as if, at a railway station, they said 'Give me a ticket,' or, in a bookshop, tendering their seven-and-sixpence, murmured, 'I want a novel.' Some of the most popular whiskies retain a vestigial character of their own, and among the products of the smaller distilleries, that are seldom met with outside Scotland, there is often a welcome individuality. But different from these as wedding-cake from a crust is the whisky one sometimes, on blessed occasions, receives from a private source: whisky of supernacular virtue, of rare and heart-taking discovery, and whisky that, under more intelligent or sympathetic legislation, could be bought without extravagance.

One such occasion I remember, when after a long journey I came in the early morning to the house of a Highland author—a man of great charm and noble character—who immediately gave me a glass from which there breathed an aroma not less distinguished and no less happy than that of an ancient brandy. It was quite different from the aroma of brandy. It was, I think, more inspiring, though perhaps less enchanting. If I may borrow a couple of words from another department of criticism it was lyrical rather than romantic. The whisky itself was equally agreeable. It was flawlessly smooth, of a very grateful and individual flavour, not full-bodied but light-hearted. Nor was it extravagantly old. It was a malt whisky, kept eleven years in wood. Its moderate age, of course, is of the utmost importance from a practical point of view, because it implies that whisky of this quality could, under equitable conditions, be produced and sold at a reasonable price.

I hesitate to mention another whisky with which I have become acquainted in Orkney, for such are its miraculous qualities that any reference to them will provoke unfair suspicion: but I have never approached it without reverence, still less in a familiar spirit. We have, in Orkney, a distiller of genius. Of the man himself I need say only this: if indeed it be true that by their fruits we may know men, then he is a good man. And of his whisky I cannot say enough. Had I the luminous wings of Shelley I might find an aërial style to praise the felicity with which it comes soaring into the ventricles of the brain. Had I the copious wordage of the good Knight of Cromarty I might say something of its bodily virtue and the great galleons of wisdom that sail upon its amber tide. Had I the point and angular precision of Euclid I might prove to a dull world the happiness within its reach.

But as it is I can say no more than the truth as it seems to a simple man: that a small cup of this whisky gives you, for a little while, the sky-borne mind of Shelley; the laughter and the fortitude of Urquhart; and the Euclidean confidence of one who has proved his theorems and solved all problems.

I hear the world crying, as it cries for its lost beatitude: Cost what it may, where can we buy this whisky?

Alas, a dragon stands before the gate of the distillery. I cannot altogether describe it, but I think it was sent there by the Exchequer. It may, perhaps, be circumvented. It might, I believe, be recalled. But St George, though he came to earth again, would not kill it, for he is an Englishman. St Andrew would be the man to scotch it.

France, I say again, has given claret to the world, and the world is the better for it. Scotland has it in its power to give to the world such whisky as few can dream of; and the world would again be better. Léoville, Margaux, and Latour might be matched with Islay, Glenfiddich and Glengrant. Haut Brion, singing aloud, might hear in reply the *voix d'or* of Highland Park. And the brown streams of Glenlivet would need not envy the sun-warmed slopes of Bordeaux. With such whisky to help it the world would grow kindlier and more wise, aware of beauty and comforted with friends.

I shall be told that the roads to-day so teem with motor-cars that it is contrary to public policy to encourage a driver to drink anything that will lift his thoughts from the stained highway before him. But why do the roads so teem with motor-cars? Why do so many people hurry to-and-fro? In pursuit of happiness, or to flee from boredom? In search of wealth, or to escape their creditors? In haste for fame, or to run from the world's noise? Remedy discontent, punish greed, cure folly, and the traffic problem will vanish, and all the world can drink in peace.

VIII

TO-DAY AND TO-MORROW

VIII

TO-DAY AND TO-MORROW

I SPEAK as a Tory, or as some kind or degree of a Tory: and an admirable statement of the Tory conception of society may be found in Lord Eustace Percy's contribution to a book entitled *Conservatism and the Future*. The statement is in two parts: first, 'that society is healthy in proportion as the greatest possible number of its members possess a recognized status not dependent upon the will of their fellow citizens;' and second, 'that no society can be healthy where the individual does not enjoy freedom of movement within the social framework, irrespective of the position in it which he occupied at birth.'

Crystallize these complementary assertions, and the emergent jewel is Freedom: freedom to stay, and freedom to go; freedom to sit and to contemplate, to create and assess, and freedom to mount and to march. But these freedoms must be mutually considerate, they must respect one another, and the marching freedom must not tread down the gardens of contemplative freedom. The individual is all-important, and the function of the State is to safeguard his security, to provide humus for his growth, and to penalize abuse of the liberty it has established.

Such a belief is not popular to-day. For yesterday and to-day men have discovered theory and practice that insistently depreciate the individual. Fascism and its unpleasant brother Hitlerism on the one hand; that well-intentioned Frankenstein, Communism, on the other; and between them, more tripes than muscle, the remnant belly of Imperialism: Imperialism dependent on an echo of the past and a growing skill in usury.

These systems variously deny or depreciate the value and status of the individual, though British Imperialism in its old age has become in many ways increasingly kind and humanitarian. It is not my business to discuss the historical background of Hitlerism; the moral indignation that palliates the brutality and futility of Communism; or the improvement in travelling facilities in Italy that in the opinion of many justifies Fascism. But the decline of British Imperialism is within the scope of my argument, for it has been accompanied by decay of the Tories' old conception of society, and overgrowth has been responsible for both decline and decay. It is true that the individual in Great Britain has still infinitely more freedom than Germans, Italians, and Russians, but the old common lands of liberty have suffered legislative encroachment in many ways; the private citizen's sense of personal responsibility has diminished; and to have freedom without responsibility is merely to live in a kind of extension of Whipsnade.

Now such is the stubborn impercipience of humanity that there may be people who will question some statements here, and so before I make the point which I am about to make—which is that the Tory conception of society can only be realized in a comparatively small society—before I state this, I had better buttress my previous assertions with a few auxiliary details. And for this purpose the interlocutory Practical Man may again be useful.

PRACTICAL MAN. You are foolishly prejudiced against Communism, Fascism, and the Nazi régime. It seems likely to me that the people of any civilized country must be capable of selecting that kind of government which suits them best; and the co-citizens of Stalin, Mussolini, and Hitler would certainly be justified not only in resenting your remarks, but in dismissing them as wanton impertinence.

LINKLATER. I form my own opinions—when I cannot find ready-made ones that suit me—and I claim the right to express them. Your assumption, moreover, that the governments we are discussing were chosen and are maintained by popular acclaim, is, I fear, unwarranted by the facts.

PRACTICAL MAN. You can't deny that all three now enjoy the enthusiastic support of the vast majority of their people.

LINKLATER. That proves nothing. In the last Grand National a horse called Golden Miller had the enthusiastic support of the vast majority of backers. But he didn't win.

PRACTICAL MAN. You gain nothing by flippancy. I would ask you seriously to consider the probability that your ideas about personal liberty—which you say are part of the Tory conception of society, but which I would describe as the Liberal view—are romantic anachronisms, and no more suited to the modern state than hansom-cabs to modern traffic conditions.

LINKLATER. Precisely. That's why I don't like the modern state. It has grown so big and so complicated that standardization of its component parts is becoming increasingly necessary—in many parts of the world habit and opinion are already like castings on a conveyor-belt in a motor-car factory—and to standardize men is to debase them. The remedy, obviously, is to abolish the necessity of standardization: that is, reduce the size and therefore the complications of the modern state. Simplify the state—but not too far: there's an optimum of simplicity—and your citizens will have a chance to become exquisitely variable, subtle, and ripe.

PRACTICAL MAN. But throughout history the tendency of the state—the successful state—has been to grow, to enlarge its boundaries, to become a complex of states, and to unite its resulting differences by imposing on them a uniformity of custom and law. That is the historical tendency, and I don't see how you can reverse it. You can't put back the clock.

LINKLATER. Why not? Hitler put back the clock when he re-introduced the executioner's axe. Mussolini put back the clock when he suppressed freedom of speech. We all put back the clock—to 1911 or thereabouts—when we began this new armaments race. It seems to me that clocks go backwards just as easily as forwards.

PRACTICAL MAN. I was talking about the whole trend of society: of humanity, if you like: and all you can find to refute my assertion is a minor trio of political expedients. Now let us ignore, for the moment, the political aspect of the matter: I merely say—and I challenge you to deny it—that man's tendency, throughout recorded history, has been to associate himself with his fellow-men, in ever-increasing numbers, for the ever-increasing satisfaction of his ever-increasing needs and desires. Evolution has created the modern state of 50,000,000 inhabitants, just as surely as evolution has created man himself. And whatever you may do to clocks, nothing can interfere with evolution.

LINKLATER. Oh, nonsense. Nature is constantly

interfering with evolution. Whenever the evolutionary tree puts out an unproductive branch, Nature comes along, diverts the sap from it, lops it off, and redirects the resultant surplus of energy elsewhere. Remember the brontosaurus. It grew too big, and its brain failed to keep pace with the growth of its body: *ergo exeunt* the brontosauruses. Now in many respects the modern state, of 50,000,000 inhabitants or so, is not unlike that doomed and superfluous dinosaur: for if you compare Great Britain of to-day with Athens in its prime you will readily perceive that though it is infinitely greater in size, the growth of its intellectual capacity has hardly been commensurate: for whereas the Athenian shopkeeper found recreation in the plays of Aristophanes, the British shopkeeper—and indeed British citizens of all classes—acquire a comparable pleasure from the flickering ephemera of the popular film. This, however, is merely a negative argument against bulk. A positive and convincing argument can be found in Viola Meynell's excellent poem called *Jonah and the Whale*. The Whale, as you may remember, had twice been wounded by harpoons: an old corroding iron was buried in his flesh, another lance stuck in his hide: but

> ' So distant were his parts that they
> Sent but a dull faint message to his brain.'

You see the likeness? In Great Britain there may be acute distress in Renfrewshire, for example, that, because of distance, ' sends but a dull faint message ' to our legislative brain in Westminster.

PRACTICAL MAN. Your Whale, I think, is little more than a Red Herring. We were discussing the social aspect of human evolution, and I had stated that mankind's historical tendency was to coalesce in ever larger political, economic, and social units. You cannot contradict that. Further, I was about to suggest—when you interrupted me—that this tendency promised most interesting developments: for as the coalescence becomes larger, it must become closer, and the increasing interdependence of individual lives may well produce, and is indeed producing, something far more vital and integrated than any existing class or society; that is to say, a communal *organism* such as the termitory on the hive. Solomon told the sluggard to go to the ant for instruction. He should have repeated his advice to historians, economists, and politicians. For with such perfection of organization before us, we can hardly doubt that the ant-hill is the true exemplar of society, and that loss of individuality is a small price to pay for such an efficient technique of living.

LINKLATER. God help you. I can't abuse you, because my store of invective is insufficient for such a case as yours. I can only reiterate my belief in the value of the individual, and repeat that small states are better than big ones, because they demand less regimentation, and so offer greater opportunity for individual freedom. No, I can do more. I can cite some distinguished authorities for my view. Aristotle, if I remember rightly, said that the supreme function of man was the soul's activity in accordance with reason: now the soul is an individual possession, reason an individual product: diminish the individual by the regimentation of the modern state of 50,000,000 inhabitants, and you circumscribe his soul, you hamstring his power of reason.

PRACTICAL MAN. I have spoken to many Nazis and Fascists—I choose them for example because regimentation is more obvious in Germany and Italy than it is here—and they all agree that under their existing régime they have a far greater freedom than ever before. They are free from doubt and anxiety.

LINKLATER. They are free from the searching of reason and the invitations of criticism. They are free to believe in what they are told, and to do what they are ordered. They are free to take their opinions off a conveyor-belt.

PRACTICAL MAN. They have voluntarily abandoned all petty preoccupation with themselves because they believe that their Race and their State are so infinitely greater than any individual, that the fate of an individual is of no consequence in comparison with the welfare of the whole.

LINKLATER. Christian teaching hardly substantiates such a view. Need I remind you of the parable about the price of two sparrows? I may be wrong, of course, in my respect for the individual, but if I am wrong I am in good company—I have already mentioned Aristotle—and I hope you will not think it presumptuous of me if I enlarge one of Dostoievsky's *obiter dicta* and say: 'I would rather be with Christ—and Aristotle—than the truth'?

PRACTICAL MAN. I don't care what company you're in. I would like to know, however, what all this has to do with England's influence on Scotland?

LINKLATER. Well, I started the chapter, very gently and tactfully, with a statement of the Tory conception of society, which I approve, and I was going to proceed to the obvious corollary that such a conception was only possible in a comparatively small society—that Great Britain, for instance, was too big for its realization, but that Scotland might well be suitable—when I realized that I had made a number of assertions which everybody might not be immediately willing to accept. So I called you in to debate them, and insensibly—but that perhaps is an invidious word—we were drawn into discussion of some wider issues.

PRACTICAL MAN. You're right when you say that some of your statements aren't likely to meet with much approval. You spoke, for example, about the decline of Great Britain: and that was simply the conventional carping of the constitutional malcontent. Britain has emerged, practically intact, from twenty years of extravagantly assorted difficulties, hardships, perils, and dilemmas. Its people have shown all the endurance, gallantry, and loyalty that we have learned to expect from them, and its rulers have displayed a most happy combination of resolution and flexibility. We have shown a far greater capacity than other peoples for dealing with the problems of world-wide depression, and having weathered the economic blizzard——

LINKLATER. We have turned the economic corner. I know, I know. There is a great deal of truth in what you say, and a good lot that is not true. But when I spoke of decline I was thinking rather of what might have been: of declining purpose; of failure to turn good into better; of shrinking, as we used not to shrink, from opportunity. For after the War—this is going to be platitudinous—Great Britain had such an opportunity for leadership as few nations have ever had. The whole earth was still full of the feeling that the War had been a war to end war, to make life safe for democracy—and *vice versa*—and to bring in a new age of decency. Great Britain had the necessary authority, experience, and apparatus to offer such leadership. We had led the world in so many ways—in war, in navigation, in trade, in administration—that surely we might have led it in a new way of peace, and liberty, and fraternity.

PRACTICAL MAN. H'm.

LINKLATER. Perhaps you're right. Anyway, we didn't. Nor did we do anything else positive or decisive. We simply managed to survive. And the reason for our failure to be positive or constructive was, I take it, much the same as the reason for our failure, during most of the War, to undertake any constructive or decisive operation on the Western Front: the armies were too large to be effectively controlled; the situation was too various to be adequately assessed; the sides of the triangle—Headquarters, Left Flank, and Right Flank—were too long; elasticity could not compete with inertia; time-lag upset the time-tables; the multiplication of possibilities of human error invalidated the power of direction; and, above all, imagination was stifled by too cumbrous circumstance, and lost in so vast an environment. Now Britain and its leaders suffer from disabilities comparable to those of the armies on the Western Front: the poor Brontosaurus, you see, with a brain no longer capable of directing so large a bulk. We failed to take a leading or formative part in the new world that shone, for a little while, wistfully on our horizon. We failed signally to make our own country —is it indecent to remind you of the phrase?—that land fit for heroes which our politicians had promised. And why? Because the Brontosaurus's poor little head had no notion what to do with the creature's huge tail, its ridiculous great haunches, its splay feet, and the enormous geography of its back. Though it moved its head into shelter, its rump stuck out in the storm. Part of it wanted to go this way, part of it was resolute to go t'other. It would clap its hands to announce a brilliant idea; but its hinderlands were asleep and didn't hear it. It sat on a cactus, but its bottom was so far from its brain that its brain didn't know it was hurt.—Are you beginning to realize the cogency of my illustration and the relevance of my disquisition?

PRACTICAL MAN. In plain words, you're saying that Britain is too large to be efficiently directed or governed?

LINKLATER. That is so. And I assume the criterion

of efficiency to be a resultant increase of human happiness.

PRACTICAL MAN. But in your chapter called *Addenda and Corrigenda* you spoke at some length about the recent benefits to Scotland of social legislation. You spoke about the humanitarian policy of successive governments. You said the labouring classes in Scotland were far better cared for than they had been. And so, presumably, they are happier than they used to be.

LINKLATER. I am trying to be fair to both sides, and that makes any argument difficult. I said that many abuses of the nineteenth century had been done away with. I said that towns were cleaner and life was healthier than it used to be. I said that many compensations were now provided for the injustices of a large industrial civilization. But the injustices remain, though they are somewhat obscured by the compensations. What recent governments have done is to palliate the diseases inherited from their predecessors.

PRACTICAL MAN. And thereby they have added to the people's happiness, and so, by your own standards, demonstrated their efficiency.

LINKLATER. They have rather soothed unhappiness. They have made the patient more comfortable. They have treated symptoms but not the disease.

PRACTICAL MAN. I'm afraid I can't waste any more time on splitting hairs. I have an important engagement elsewhere.

LINKLATER. Well, I intend to stay here for some considerable time yet. But I hope you have a good round. Good-bye!

My point, I think, is obvious: the most unfortunate result of Scotland's association with England has been the immersion of Scotland in a modern brontosaurian state of nearly 50,000,000 inhabitants. A state, that is, too large to permit the realization of the old Tory conception of society, that conception being the political corollary of a truth recognized by, and fundamental in, the two greatest cultures known to mankind, the Greek and the Christian.

It was Rupert Brooke, I think, who said, in some letter, that of all men poets were the most practical; and if you will call a poet by his old Scots name of *makar*, then a novelist is cater-cousin to him, for he too makes, and, making, must be practical. And so, being practical, I say that little nations are, in the way of nations, all that men can happily make.

A nation needs laws: and who can legislate for fifty million, save by the methods of Procrustes, that first apostle of standardization? A nation needs care: but a nation of fifty million souls is a patchwork of conflicting elements, and who can care for the interests of one save at the expense of others? A nation needs happiness: but positive happiness depends, first and last, on spiritual security, and the spirit is lost and deafened in the noise and complexities and bitter extravagance of the modern state. A nation needs sanity: but what chance for sanity is there when nine out of every ten people are, by the very facts of their existence, irremediably and so remotely dissociated from the natural processes of production, from the growth of the soil, and the harvesting of the sea? To contemplate these is to perceive at once the sobriety and the danger of life, its labour and its gaiety, and in the balance of these perceptions lies the generous foundation of sanity. But when the life of twenty million people is conditioned solely by the artificial productivity of a factory—a germination that none of them observes, a germination killed or stimulated by political repercussions beyond their comprehension or control—what chance of sanity have they? What prospects of sanity reach the vision of the two or three million whose life is the notation or calculation of profit and loss on the exchange of currencies that have lost their value, commodities that exist only to satisfy an artificial demand, products of a labour they do not understand, and the fructification of a growth they have never seen? Many of these are protected from insanity by a natural obtuseness: the ostrich is not the only creature to bury its head in the sand. Others acquire a protective cynicism, and these, the dog-toothed grinners, are truly brave. But positive sanity, in a large modern state, is rare as chastity in the Trobriand Islands.

Now it may be—I do not deny the possibilities, though I cannot favour them—it may be that I have created a false impression, and adopted a poor standard of values. I have, to begin with, not the slightest intention of glorifying a culture whose sole foundations are the spinning-wheel and the plough. I have merely said that sanity ultimately depends on some apprehension of the circumstances and forces of natural production; and deprecated the inevitable and remote dissociation from such awareness of the bulk of the population in a modern state. I have been pleading, at least by implication, for a community large enough to include all kinds of human activity, mental, spiritual, and physical; yet small enough to give everyone, in some degree, the opportunity to appreciate the nature of his fellow-citizens' vocations.

In the second place my assumption of the enduring human-background-importance of agriculture may, apparently, be challenged by the recent history of farming and the present theory and experimentation of certain scientists. Since 1850 the agricultural population of the world has, it is estimated, decreased by fifty million people: but not at the expense of production. Production has grown like a giant on scientific knowledge and the scientific use of phosphates and new seed mixtures, wild white clover and ingenious machinery. In some parts of Scotland the production of beef per acre has already been doubled.[1] The virility of the modern oat would startle Ceres, and Chaucer's gentle cock would pale—coral comb and azure legs and colour of burnt gold would all go pale —to see the fecundity of the fashionable hen. Yet while the fruits of the earth grow more, the tillers of the earth and the gardeners of the fruit grow less. And to this fact we are already reconciled. Reconciled? We are justly proud of it, for we grow better by no mean but we have made that mean. Now, however, come theory and experiment, like detonator and grenade, to shatter any belief we may entertain that progress, in agriculture at least, is safe and slow. For Dr Willcox of Iowa has recently stated that two hundred and twenty-five bushels of maize have been produced from one acre of ground [1] —ten times the average yield of maize in the United

---

[1] For these and neighbouring facts—though not opinions—I am indebted to a paper by Sir Robert Greig, sometime Secretary to the Department of Agriculture; and for permission to quote them I am again obliged to him.

States—by virtue of his discovery that the soil is hardly more than an excuse for using fertilizers; and arising out of this, and comparable experiments on other staple crops, comes the calculation that, with no more than existing knowledge, and with favourable conditions and adequate management, staple foods for the whole earth could be grown in the basin of the Mississippi River. . . .

Alas for small nations, and alas for little farms! Government after government, competing against this monstrous output, will ruin itself with subsidies to wheat and beet and meat. Silk and milk will be born in charity, grain and sugar-cane exist on vails. And eleemosynary ham and lamb will quarrel for places in the national workhouse with dole-grown strawberry jam. Then at last, bankrupt at last, the nations will bow to the preposterous benevolence of the Mississippi; and pay for it through the nose. . . .

That, perhaps, is the first picture to be excited by the marriage of Demeter and Dr Willcox. A vision comes of plough-land everywhere going back to grass, and grass to bracken; of farmers vanishing like the dodo and the diplodocus; of good growing lands deserted by all but picnic-parties and painters in water-colour. But the vision soon fades. It dies at the cold approach of politics and economics; for the Mississippi, no matter what it could do, will in fact grow no more than may find a profitable market. And the world, rejecting the embarrassing beneficence of Old Man River, will take good care that few markets are available. But when that vision has faded, another, no less alarming, comes in its place. For if Dr Willcox's knowledge becomes common property, and such practice becomes common practice, then even the smallest country may become self-supporting. And that, in the peculiar economy of our time, is a terrifying thought.

If Britain grew all its own food—Norfolk wheat, Aberdeenshire beef, Hereford apples, Border sheep, and eggs dropping like hail in every backyard from Bristol to Wick—if Britain bought no food from overseas, what would Denmark and New Zealand, Canada and the Argentine do then, poor things? They would close their accounts with British manufacturers, in the first place. For economists agree—and they may be right for once—that if we do not buy, we cannot sell. And so, being unable to sell abroad, we should suffer poverty in the midst of plenty. That, of course, taking the world as a whole, is roughly our condition to-day. But to-morrow it may be the separate condition of every nation.

New methods in agriculture—Dr Willcox's and others—promise and produce a surplus of food. New mechanical devices produce a surplus of made goods. In both cases the surplus remains a surplus because the potential consumers cannot afford to buy it. That is to say, the problem of distribution has not yet been solved. And while the problem grows more complicated by the addition of productive factors, the solution becomes more remote by the subtraction of the consumers' wealth. What, then, is to be done? Shall we find contentment in the contemplation of such irony? Irony is not popular in Britain.

The weapon necessary to tackle the problem is a pair of scissors. Cut it into intelligible and therefore manageable fragments. Even after radical division, however, the problem would still be difficult. No mere economist would ever solve it. A new philosophy, a new conception of wealth, and a more reasonable understanding of happiness would be necessary. But in so small a place as Scotland that new philosophy could be more easily put into practice than in so large a place as Great Britain. It could be applied to Brittany or to Provence more conveniently than to France as a whole. It could be more efficiently adapted to conditions in Bavaria than to the multiform conditions of all Germany. California and Louisiana could use it to suit themselves with less argument and ill-nature than could the forty-eight States in undivided union. There is more wisdom than cynicism in *Divide and rule*.

Now people of an opposite opinion to mine—people who desire the progressive internationalization of the world, the abolition of frontiers, and more and more unity—are fond of deprecating nationalism on the ground that it fosters enmities, hostile competition, and a habit of jealous isolation. This erroneous belief is due to their confusion of nationalism with imperialism. It is the great empires and not the little nations that threaten the peace of the world. Germany and Japan are obviously more of a menace to us all than are Norway and Sweden. Italy is more jealous of her totalitarian honour than Denmark. And isolation has its most notorious advocate in Lord Beaverbrook, a citizen of the British Commonwealth.

Surely it is obvious that internationalism is possible only if there exists a sufficient number of nations to make it worth while? Surely it is apparent that with a larger number of nations there would be more possibilities of international contact? And if every country were smaller its neighbours would be nearer.

But let us recapitulate, and conclude the chapter with a fable:

Imperialism is simply the homologue of growing-up. The building of empires is the world's method of putting on its first long trousers—for though the Hittites built an empire a few thousand years ago, a few thousand years is but a fraction of the time required for a biological or social-evolutionary experiment, and little real advance can be looked for in so short a time: the Hittites were infant prodigies and died young.

Empire-building is, of course, only the largest and most spectacular indication of this natural desire to simulate growing-up by growing big. The department store, the mammoth newspaper with its boast of a huge circulation—'Yah! I'm bigger than you are!'—the skyscrapers of Chicago (though these have an æsthetic justification), the modern state that tries to make a corporative giant out of little individuals —these things and many more are homologous to the lanky sprouting of a boy or the addition to a tree's circumference of its annual ring. But they have no intrinsic merit, and they will disappear when the world is truly an adult world. There is no point in growing more when one is grown-up.

If there is any lesson at all to be learnt from the last twenty years, it is surely that bigness has few virtues. The last war was a big war—so big that no one could manage it: no one could win it, and it was almost impossible to lose it. Old theories of strategy, built on the handling of small professional forces, were useless. The armies grew larger and larger, and no one knew what to do with them. Company commanders, it is true, were often very efficient people; brigadiers were rather less efficient; divisional generals were constantly at fault; and army commanders were seldom able to control the movements of their troops according to plan. Efficiency diminished as the machine grew greater. And after the War financial and commercial undertakings of all kinds continued to prove this: banks, shipping companies, match factories, petroleum companies, and a hundred other concerns increased their deposits, production, turnover or what-not until, like the Allied armies in the field, they became quite unmanageable, and finally outdid the statistics of their mushroom wealth with the size of their casualty lists.

The insoluble economic problems of the modern state are largely due to the unmanageable size of the modern state, that is full of contradictory desires and antipathetic interests. You can't lower the price of beef without offending the butchers, and there are so many butchers in a civilized country that no politician dares offend them. You can't raise the producers' price without cutting the profits of half a million middlemen, and cutting their profits would reduce their purchasing power, and throw shirt-makers and golf-caddies and restaurateurs out of work, as well as diminishing the Chancellor's receipts from income tax. You can't raise the tariff on French potatoes and claret to help Australian vignerons and English market-gardeners without the French docking their coal imports and so depriving colliery shareholders of their ability to buy English new potatoes and a bottle of Emu burgundy. Mr MacDonald's government—or M. Daladier-Herriot-Boncour-Chautemps-Flandin's—or Mr Roosevelt's—can no more help one section of the community without hurting several others, than General Blank could order the 1st Brackens, the 1st Loamshires, the 2nd Canutes and the 5th Sessex to take Mont Jemenfiche without running the Brackens into uncut wire and leaving the

Canutes in a wholly indefensible salient. The bigger they are the harder they fall—and they fall more frequently.

Size, then, reduces efficiency. It also reduces the political amenities: that is to say it increases the possible minority and therefore the possible discontent. There is, let us say, a big country called Magnolia with an adult population of 4000 all enjoying the suffrage. In Magnolia it is possible to find a political minority numbering 1999. But ethnologically there are four distinct peoples in Magnolia, and after some discussion they agree to separate and set up four independent states. Each of these states has an adult population of 1000, all enjoying the suffrage. The largest possible minority in each of them is 499—and so the largest possible total of minorities in Magnolia becomes 1996, a reduction of three on the old figures. That is to say: in the four small new countries it is impossible, at the worst of times, to have so much political discontent as, on the worst occasions, there was in the old empire of Magnolia. (I assume a democratic principle of government, of course.) In other words, every individual in the little new countries has a larger chance of contentment, a larger chance of getting his wishes attended to, and is naturally of increased value to the state, and so to himself, in proportion to the numerical decrease of its population.

Let us continue the story of Magnolia. Magnolia had a neighbour, a peace-loving country called Diffidentia. Now, in the old days Diffidentia was always afraid of the great power of Magnolia, and so taxed its people heavily to pay for armaments and a large military establishment. But when Magnolia divided itself into four, none of the new little states could afford to buy anything more than machine-guns and other strictly defensive weapons. (The Magnolian Armament Factory, indeed, went out of business, and was reconstituted as Superior Household Plumbing, Ltd.) Seeing this, Diffidentia also disarmed, and the consequent reduction of Diffidential taxation brought increased domestic prosperity, and Diffidentia was able —it never had been before—to import excellent mahogany furniture, admirable applejack, most nutritive ground nuts, and very imposing marble tombstones, the special productions of the four quarters of Magnolia, to the great satisfaction of Diffidentia and to the great profit and contentment of the four states of Magnolia.

Now I do not want this story to be simply a politico-geographical idyll. Difficulties must not be forgotten, and it happens that Magnolia's other neighbour was a truculent *arriviste* republic called Malevolenz. When Magnolia split into four Malevolenz adopted a bullying attitude, made impossible demands, and delivered ultimatums of the most alarming kind to the four new states, in which for some time there was considerable trepidation. But fortunately Malevolenz also had neighbours: the great empires of Gargaphie and Drax: and in obedience to the new political movement of Benevolent Dissociation (as it was called), Gargaphie and Drax had recently split up into a dozen small principalities, all of which bought much of their household coal from Malevolenz.

The four states of Magnolia took their troubles to Geneva and found ready sympathy from the representatives of the Gargaphie-Drax principalities; being themselves representatives of small states they were naturally sympathetic with the difficulties of other small states. As a result of their conference all the Gargaphie-Drax governments sent simultaneous notices to Malevolenz, stating that unless the ultimatums were immediately withdrawn, they, the independent peoples of the late empires of Gargaphie and Drax, would cease to buy coal from Malevolenz and would burn Irish peat instead. On receipt of this information

Malevolenz, grumbling a good deal it is true, withdrew her ultimatums within forty-eight hours.

Nor is the story ended. At one time—but this was a long time ago, when Europe was first discovered by the Americans—Magnolia, Gargaphie, and Drax had been much visited by American tourists, who delighted in their individual cultures, their sturdy peasantry, their colourful dress, and their ability to remain different from the rest of the world. But in the course of time Magnolia, Gargaphie, and Drax had succumbed—partly as a result of American influence—to the modern craze for uniformity, and had gradually become almost indistinguishable from any other part of the world. The Americans then ceased to visit them, for they could find cinemas, soda-fountains, 40/- suits, and Birmingham jewellery in Kansas City, Minnesota, and Oakland, without the discomfort and expense of a preliminary sea-voyage. Gargaphie, Drax, and Magnolia thereby suffered a serious loss of income, and the Americans suffered an even more serious loss of interest in the world, which, they said, was becoming very flat and tasteless.

But a few years after the Benevolent Dissociation there reappeared in the new states of Gargaphie, Drax, and Magnolia all their old traditional costumes, their native cultures, their own songs and dances and forms of local government, and a new and stronger life inspired them. Every citizen in those new little states was of more importance than he had been when a multitude of fellow-citizens obscured his identity; and because of this resurgent individuality the arts flourished, and flourished with a fine disregard for the fashions of neighbouring states. In this way the theatres in Eastern Gargaphie had dramatic theories entirely different from those in Western Gargaphie; the painters in Southern Magnolia used a wholly different technique from that of the painters in Northern Magnolia; and the poets of Drax-in-the-Mountains all composed exquisite lyric poetry, while the poets in Drax-by-the-Sea brought forth enormous and magnificent epics.

Because of this infinite variety within their boundaries, Drax, Magnolia, and Gargaphie became the favourite resorts of tens of thousands of English, American, German, and Russian tourists, who brought prosperity with them and returned to their own countries with infinite gratitude to God—and to Gargaphie, Drax, and Magnolia—for this revelation of the manifold talents and delicious eccentricity of mankind, and straightway split up their own ridiculously large and dull countries into little interesting ones, with the result that the world became a place where, though other ills certainly persisted, no one ever complained of monotony or boredom or had nightmares about imperialistic steam-rollers.

This, I think, is a pleasant story. But unlike many pleasant stories it is not quite so impossible of realization as most people will believe. The chief obstacle to its realization is that a world of little countries, with proper machinery to control the flow or flight of capital, would give rich men fewer opportunities to become millionaires, and millionaires no chance at all to become billionaires. And the desire for riches is at present an influence even more dominating than Stalin, Mussolini, Kemal, and the people behind Hitler. But the passion to get as much as you can and get it quickly was not always humanity's dominating motive: the doctrine of the fair price held considerable sway in the Middle Ages, and the pride of the craftsman has done more for the world than the financier's pride will ever do. A 'change of heart' is not impossible in the world—it would come more easily if a happier phrase described it—and a change of heart can bring about any kind of revolution.

IX
THE TENTATIVE CONCLUSION

IX

THE TENTATIVE CONCLUSION

Now to what conclusion can one come as a result of these small enquiries, this gentle exploration, and tentative dissection? I am tempted to write *Nescio* and be done with it. But though there would be some truth in that answer, there would also be a lot of untruth. For even after writing of the inter-action and inter-relations of England and Scotland—and the speediest way to realize one's ignorance of a subject is to essay a book upon it—I still feel I know a good deal about them.

There is one thing that may be said without chance of contradiction: and that is, that our incorporation in Great Britain has been of great material benefit to very many individual Scotsmen. It has enormously increased their opportunities of becoming rich, famous, or even happy. Commercial success, a career in politics, or superior social amenities have been England's gift to innumerable invading Scots.

Gift, however, is the wrong word. Our south-going countrymen have worked hard for whatever

THE TENTATIVE CONCLUSION

success they may have gained, and though England provided a convenient field for their efforts, it cannot be said that the enfeoffment was gratuitous. One must suppose that their services were needed—their engineering, their accountancy, their soldiering and therapy—and that whatever reward they acquired was duly earned. 'The unicellular plants called Algae are adopted by marine creatures called Radiolarians, whose nitrogenous waste they consume and for whom they liberate oxygen.'[1] A very great deal of oxygen has been liberated for England by the Scottish algae, and presumably England is the better for it.

For two hundred years the Scottish regiments have been of inestimable service to imperial England, and from the Highlands in particular the Army has always recruited an extraordinarily high percentage of the available man-power, except during a period following the Clearances. 'In the forty years after 1797, *Skye alone* gave the British Army 21 Lieutenant-Generals and Major-Generals, 48 Lieutenant-Colonels, 600 Majors, Captains, and Subalterns, and 10,000 private soldiers; and to the Civil Service in the same time, one Governor-General of India, four Governors of Colonies, a Chief Baron of England, and a Lord of Session.'[2]

---

[1] Chapter I.
[2] Agnes Mure Mackenzie: *An Historical Survey of Scottish Literature*.

THE TENTATIVE CONCLUSION

The Governors and the Generals did well out of the symbiosis, but it is improbable that Skye's 10,000 private soldiers got from it much more material profit than a few years of army rations, a handsome uniform, and ninepence a day if they were disabled. The army was their natural vocation, of course, and military service suited them. But if there had been no English recruiting officers they could have found service on as good terms with any one of half-a-dozen continental powers; whereas England would have looked in vain for such able mercenaries. For centuries Scotland had provided the continent with admirable troops, and but for the Union Scots could still have sold their swords —or rifles—in open market. When England obtained a monopoly of this notable recruiting area, it was England, not Scotland, that felt the benefit.

Consider also the great number of Scots who have held administrative office under the Crown. Read the history of Colonial expansion, and look for Scottish names: they are numerous as herring-scales on an old fishing-boat. The vast majority of those men acquired office by their own ability and held it by their own merit. Now it is the way of things that a good servant is more profitable to his master than to himself; and so these servants of the Crown benefited the Crown, which is predominantly English, more than they benefited themselves. Yet doubtless their employment satisfied them—it was honourable and reasonably remunerative—and they were indebted for it to the Anglo-Scottish symbiosis.

On a lower stratum of society there are the many Scottish footballers who have been hired by English clubs. Their wages are good, their vocation is popular, and they are presumably well pleased to be playing for Chelsea or the Arsenal. They also owe their livelihood to the Anglo-Scottish symbiosis. But football clubs are commercial bodies, and if Sandy McCentre is paid £5 a week to play for an English team we may safely assume that its directors expect him to increase its gate-money by—let us be moderate—five guineas.

Between footballers and Governors of Colonies there is resident in England a mixed crowd of Scottish gardeners, engineers, doctors, accountants, government officials and others who serve public authority or the community, and, by the same reasoning, benefit that authority or community—which is entirely or predominantly English—more than they benefit themselves. And Scotland, that gave them birth, receives from their efforts no direct benefit at all.

True, Scotland benefits indirectly by the appreciation of British or Imperial Stock, in which she is a minor shareholder. But to maintain the rate of

THE TENTATIVE CONCLUSION

interest she is constantly exporting more capital—her manhood—and for some considerable time there have been signs that the drainage is adversely affecting her health.

Let us return to the statement that Scotland's incorporation in Great Britain has been of great material benefit to very many individual Scotsmen. Despite the argument that a good servant's profit is always less than his master's, that statement is true. But by the very fact that individual Scots have profited from the symbiosis, Scotland as a whole, as a nation, has suffered: for she has lost not only the master's profit that she might have expected from her own sons, but in great numbers her sons themselves. They have gone to England or to the Dominions, and taken their talents with them. It is true that Scotland could not have found employment for them all; but she could have found employment for more than are left to her, and, had she been a sovereign power, for many who deserted her because their abilities were too great to find satisfaction in a provincial estate. The southward and outward trend, not merely of industry but of intellect, is too obvious to need argument. It cannot be denied; and no matter how large may be its indirect profits, it can hardly be maintained that a nation is likely to retain its strength, far less gain new strength, when the tendency of its most able and energetic people is so persistently centrifugal.

It may be said, of course, that the decay of Scotland is a matter of no importance. It may be said that Scotland the political entity—or shadow of an entity—is of no value to the world to-day. It may be argued that the virtue of Scotland exists only in Scots men and women, and persists in them wherever they may be. (One remembers that our ancient rulers were crowned, not King of Scotland, but King of Scots.) Our sense of patriotism, like that of the Jews, may be racial, not local. But even if this be admitted, there is still the difficulty of maintaining an established type from depleted stock. If you own a herd of prize cattle you can make a lot of money by selling all your best bulls to the Argentine; but you will not improve your own calves by such a policy.

I do not wish to over-state the case and give the impression that Scotland is now inhabited only by weaklings. An abundance of physical energy remains. —A young American woman, who had travelled there, once said to me: 'Why, that darned country's just lousy with good-looking men.'—And a little while ago I saw in Edinburgh a sight that filled me with happiness and relief. For in a novel called *Magnus Merriman* I had written of the magnificent spectacle

THE TENTATIVE CONCLUSION

that Edinburgh makes when Princes Street is filled with the people who go to see the Rugby Internationals at Murrayfield. I had praised, in somewhat overflowing language, the thews and the strength of the men, the girls' tall figures and their fine complexions. And a year later I wondered if I had overdone it. I thought uncomfortably that perhaps I had romanticized that cheerful crowd, and this year, on the morning of the match for the Calcutta Cup, I went timidly to Princes Street, expecting disillusion. But as surely as the Castle sits on a rock, the young men and women were even taller and stronger and lovelier than I had said they were; and the somewhat flamboyant passage in *Magnus Merriman* was merely an interesting example of understatement. Edinburgh is still a good place to live in; but how much better it might be! That Gothic mile, from the Castle to Holyroodhouse, deserves a race of heroes; and the New Town should be peopled by wit and culture, by urbanity and beauty. The physique is there, and so is beauty. But a handful of anecdotes will pass for wit, and culture is shy, and short of breath, and rare at that.

In Aberdeen, too, there is great physical vigour, and behind those granite walls, that make of it a place as secret as an Oriental town, hospitality and entertainment may rise to a glorious robustitude. But intellectually the people are lifeless, and old habits of thought, worn smooth as Victorian ha'pennies with the passage of time, will readily pass as opinion bright and new-minted. The people survive, but they do not seek. They are comfortable, not curious. Most of them stay at home, which is for Scotland's good, and they keep their minds there too, which is hardly so valuable; but many have gone to feed Malaya and the Civil Service, the Canadian universities and the Indian Police. Like the rest of Scotland, their principal export has been manpower.

But why for evermore should the ends of the earth be nourished at Scotland's expense? Is it beauty the young men go out to seek? There is beauty in the Highlands to match the Vale of Kashmir. Is it honourable work? There would be more merit in rebuilding Glasgow than in levelling the Andes. Is it salaries and a pension? There is work at home that would bring a more lasting reward.

I know the answer to that, of course: no such work could be set afoot without political power to authorize and direct and finance it. And that takes us back to Scottish Nationalism and the debate of Small Nations versus Great Nations, and confronts me with another of those seeming contradictions that are the bane of those who deal in generalizations. For I have

THE TENTATIVE CONCLUSION

spoken of the work that cries to be done in Scotland, and now I want to speak of leisure, for which I have a most tender regard. And notwithstanding the work of reconstruction that would face any small nation newly emergent from the complex of a great nation, the small nations are the true protagonists of leisure, and leisure is recognized by the sociologists as one of the several indices of a true civilization.

It is, I know, becoming a platitude to say that we must all prepare ourselves for the many difficulties of living in partial idleness. Our elder statesmen and our younger economists combine to prophesy a grateful otium. They look with some displeasure at our toil-worn hands and industrious habits, and tell us that we must learn the arts of *dolce far niente*. But are they speaking the truth? For the more they talk of coming leisure, the harder, it seems to me, do people work. I was talking the other day to a young man who is going to be a chartered accountant. His whole day is occupied with university classes and office work, and his every evening is spent in study. This routine, which no trade union would allow, he must pursue for six long years —and all to be a chartered accountant. I wouldn't work as hard as that to become a chartered libertine.

Another friend of mine, a medical student, tells me that he studies every night of the week till 12 o'clock,

THE TENTATIVE CONCLUSION

and that this is absolutely necessary to cover the prescribed work. Now once upon a time I was a medical student myself, but I never contemplated the possibility of such slavery as that. It is true that I rarely passed any examinations, but many of my friends were more successful, and none of them, so far as I know, submitted to such inhuman thraldom. This passionate addiction to work is a new growth, and it hardly substantiates the popular prediction of coming leisure.

Nor are these isolated examples. Look at the morning crowd of workers on their way to office, shop, and factory; they should be strolling leisurely, amiably chattering, stopping here and there to flirt or argue, intermitting their journey at café or pub for a cup of coffee or a glass of beer. But are they? Not a bit of it. They tear along as though they were training for athletic sports.

For the last half-century ingenious and pitifully wrong-headed men have been inventing and making millions of tons of machinery that is said to be labour-saving; and the result of their altruism is that the working-day of the more obviously working-classes in London has been shortened by one hour. Good, you say. But in that period the number of workmen in London has doubled, or trebled, or perhaps quadrupled—I am not very good at figures—and most of

THE TENTATIVE CONCLUSION

them now live so far from their work that they need an hour to get to it and another hour to return. Labour-saving machinery has its purpose and its use, but the saving of labour is neither. It exists to bear the unnecessary burden of millions of people with whom you are needlessly associated, to mitigate the obvious inconveniencies of that undesirable association, and to extract from it an anti-social superfluity of wealth for the controlling minority. In a small state, freed from the task of transporting, directing, feeding, healing, sanitating and exploiting unwanted millions, labour-saving machinery would rust and perish; and that would indeed save labour, for it would no longer need the service of its myriad attendants; and being no longer mulcted for its upkeep of four shillings and sixpence in the pound, we could idle for eight or ten weeks out of the nearly twelve—twelve weeks in every year! Who said the corvée was abolished?—during which we work only to feed the Exchequer.

And sunk like Atlantis beneath the tides of time is that sweet tradition of Government servants who worked like gentlemen from ten till four, and from that submerged quarter of the day raised for their recreation a broad two hours for lunch. Buried like Chaldean cities is the gentle notion that your women of the upper classes need do no work but fancy work, and cultivate no art but the arts to please a husband.— You say they work because they want to, and because at last they are independent? Fiddlesticks, ma'am. Fiddlesticks and nodulated bosh. They work because a great new burden of toil has been found, and someone must bear it.

The suspicion rises that, so far from leisure being imminent, civilization is becoming so complicated that we shall have to work harder and ever harder to keep it in running order. Everyone knows the sort of house that is so full of ornaments, knick-knacks, and gadgets, that mistress and maids are for ever dusting, cleaning, and re-arranging. Everyone knows that a motor-car costing £1500 requires a lot more looking after than a modest roadster that costs £150. And we cannot escape the fear that our present civilization increasingly resembles that opulent motor-car and that overcrowded house.

I see, then, in my Small Nation, this seemingly contradictory association of sufficing work and ample leisure. Call them complementary or alternative as you please. In a truly efficient civilization, which a small civilization might be, it should be possible to provide work for those who like it, and leisure for those who don't. Any amiable village will give an example of this most humane division of labour. It

THE TENTATIVE CONCLUSION

requires a tolerant spirit, of course. But it is surely easier to be tolerant with people when you are in personal contact with them, than when you are dealing with masses from afar. There are exceptions to this rule, of course, but systematic intolerance is always connected with remote authority, and the converse is nearly as true.

But if I say too much about leisure I shall be suspected of flippancy, as surely as if I pause again to speak common sense about human happiness I shall be accused of sentimentality; and, for the moment, I would like to be thought serious. . . .

Let us return to our native mutton: to the Scotsmen who have profited by the incorporation in Britain; to the England that has benefited by a recruiting area and the master's share of the profits; to the Scotland that has exported too much human capital, and has gained, in return for its Imperial investment, a considerable income of amenities. In the more recent development of their relations, this benevolence to individuals and diminishment to the nation has been England's largest meaning for Scotland. Whether the diminishment will continue is not yet clear. Scottish Nationalists say no. But their chorus, though fervent, is small in volume. The majority of people in Scotland either deny the diminishment—as sleepy schoolboys

THE TENTATIVE CONCLUSION

will resolutely deny that it is time to get up—or ignore it. But despite the inertia of the mass the reiterated negative of the Nationalist minority has not been without effect, and there is assuredly a greater consciousness of nationality in Scotland to-day than there was thirty years ago.

History, moreover, would seem to be on the side of the Nationalists, for a quality of resurgence has been so regular a characteristic of Scotland as to appear, if not inevitable, at least normal. Scotsmen have, in recent memory, reclaimed elsewhere a poorer soil than many deer-forests, enriched less noble rivers than the Clyde, and ruled people as intractable as Lowland Presbyterians. If some breath of wisdom decides us to do for ourselves what we have done for others, Scotland will again play a part in the world, and find for its own people a worthy and congenial life at home. Our little renaissance, that we discuss so earnestly, and our new politics, that do not yet interest many, may be the prelude to a new era. It will require some expert readjustment to begin with, but devolution is only another phase of evolution, and the experiment should be interesting. As Agnes Mure Mackenzie has charmingly said: *Il faut cultiver notre chardon.*